20T10

Church and Nation

Faith and the Future
General Editor: David Nicholls

Choices
Ethics and the Christian
David Brown

Church and Nation
Peter Cornwell

Pastoral Care and the Parish
Peter Davie

The Faith Abroad
John D. Davies

Church, Ministry and Unity
A Divine Commission
James E. Griffiss

The Authority of Divine Love
Richard Harries

The Bible
Fountain and Well of Truth
John Muddiman

Faith, Prayer and Devotion
Ralph Townsend

Sacraments and Liturgy
The Outward Signs
Louis Weil

Church and Nation

Peter Cornwell

Basil Blackwell

Peter Cornwell 1983

First published 1983
Basil Blackwell Publisher Limited
108 Cowley Road, Oxford OX4 1JF, England

British Library Cataloguing in Publication Data

Cornwell, Peter
  Church and nation.—(Faith and the future)
  1. Church of England
  I. Title   II. Series
  262'.03'42   BX5131.2

  ISBN 0-631-13223-6
  ISBN 0-631-13224-4 Pbk

Typesetting by Cambrian Typesetters,
Aldershot, Hants
Printed in Great Britain by
T.J. Press Ltd, Padstow

Contents

Foreword

This book is one of a series whose writers consider some important aspects of Christianity in the contemporary scene and in so doing draw inspiration from the Catholic revival in the Anglican Communion which began in Oxford one hundred and fifty years ago. This revival — with its thinkers, pastors, prophets, social reformers and not a few who have been held to be saints — has experienced changes in the understanding of the Christian faith since the time of the Tractarians and has none the less borne witness to themes which are deep and unchanging. Among these are the call to holiness, the communion of saints, the priesthood of the Church and its ministers and a sacramental religion, both otherworldly, and with revolutionary claims upon man's social life

I am myself convinced that the renewal of the Church for today and tomorrow needs a deep recovery of these themes of Catholic tradition and a vision of their contemporary application. The books of this series are designed towards this end, and I am sure that readers will be grateful for the help they give. Many are thirsty but 'the well is deep'.

+ Michael Ramsey

1 Establishment — Dead or Alive?

The event which has been considered the beginning of the Oxford Movement, John Keble's Assize Sermon on 14 July 1833, focused on the relationship between the Church of England and the nation. The issue, the suppression of the Irish bishoprics by Parliament, seems absurdly trivial. To reduce the number of bishops in this minority church made good reforming sense, and yet the issue which Keble raised, the right of Parliament to reform the church as it were over that church's head, proved to be more than trivial. Could this mouthpiece of the nation be trusted to reform the church aright, when all the evidence suggested that the nation no longer adhered to those 'apostolical' principles to which Keble and his friends were recalling the church? Keble, far from stirring up a conflict between church and state, believed that he was simply drawing attention to a conflict which already existed. The beliefs of church and nation had come to diverge.

Our subject is the relationship of a particular church to a particular nation. By thus narrowing down what is a vast subject we shall appear parochial and perhaps unaware of those areas in the world where the relationship of church to nation causes greater anxiety. Where the shoe really pinches is in Latin America, South Africa and Poland, rather than in England. Yet by concentrating on what is known and familiar, we may be in a better position to sympathize with other Christians plunged into situations of more overt conflict. Moreover, if change and reform are called for it is best that they should begin at home with the casting out of planks from our own eyes, rather than with attempting to remove specks from the eyes of others. And yet we must avoid the danger of making it appear that the problems which Keble exposed are peculiar to our situation. That tension between church and nation is but one aspect of the continuing tension between the church and the world which reaches back into the pages of the New Testament. Christians are called to adhere to the startling values of the kingdom of God and yet to do this without being withdrawn from the world. Indeed they are to be in the world as light, salt and leaven, creatively contributing to its life by their distinctive beliefs and pattern of life. Jesus says in St John's Gospel:

> I do not pray that thou shouldest take them out of the world, but that thou shouldest keep them from the evil one. They are not of the world, even as I am not of the world. Sanctify them in the truth, thy word is truth. As thou didst send me into the world, so I have sent them into the world. And for their sake I consecrate myself that they also may be consecrated in truth. (John 17:15–19) RSV

This, for all time, states the relationship of Christians to the world and so to the nations of the world: not withdrawn but creatively present because set apart, consecrated in the truth which is Christ the Word of God.

Christianity from its beginning thus rejected a world-denying sectarianism. Despite the fact that the established religion of the Roman empire was pagan, the Church nevertheless had a high doctrine of the state. 'There is no authority except from God and those that exist have been instituted by God.' The ruler, although a pagan, is 'God's servant for your good'. Therefore, not simply because it is prudent, but also for conscience's sake one must 'pay all of them their dues, taxes to whom taxes are due, revenue to whom revenue is due, respect to whom respect is due, honour to whom honour is due' (Romans 13:7). Thus the involvement of Christians in society is emphasized in a second-century letter by an unknown writer:

The distinction between Christians and other men is neither in country nor language nor customs. For they do not dwell in cities in some place of their own, nor do they use any strange variety of dialect, nor practise any extraordinary kind of life. [They follow] the local customs both in clothing and food and in the rest of life. (Epistle to Diognetus 5)

With this conformity and insistence on ordinariness there goes however a deep rooted nonconformity. If for the world there are lords many, for the Christian there is one Lord Jesus Christ 'the only Sovereign, the King of kings, and Lord of lords'. (Timothy 6:15). Although on Calvary the world rejects him, there his lordship is won as 'he disarmed the principalities and powers and made a public example of them, triumphing over them in him' (Colossians 2:15). The kingdoms of this world are now destined to become the kingdom of our Christ. It is right to give the coin marked with the emperor's head back to the emperor, but we are marked with the image and likeness of God and thus must give ourselves to God alone. The absolute state which demands what is due to God is dethroned, so that, when it comes to the sharp and painful choice, we must obey God rather than men. Not even the innocent-seeming pinch of incense could be offered to Caesar. The state which thus demands my soul, my life, my all, becomes in the Book of Revelation the Beast, the Anti-Christ. This nonconformity was no mere individual eccentricity; it was the threatening nonconformity of an identifiable group, so that when, on the fairly rare occasions that the persecution of Christians was turned from being the result of mob violence into official state policy, they were hounded not for their beliefs, but for belonging to the sort of alternative society to which the Roman authorities were so sensitive. The perceived danger was the presence of an identifiable group which refused the empire's bond of unity, the worship offered to its head. Thus together with the insistence of the Epistle to Diognetus on the full participation of Christians in society, there goes the equal insistence on the wonderful and confessedly strange character of their own citizenship . . . They dwell in their own fatherlands but as if sojourners in them, they share all things as citizens and suffer all things as strangers. Every foreign country is their fatherland and every fatherland is a foreign country. (Epistle to Diognetus 5)

This reflects the belief expressed in 1 Peter that the Church is 'a chosen race, a royal priesthood, a holy nation, God's own people' (1 Peter 2:9) and thus that Christians are present in the world as 'aliens and exiles' (1 Peter 2:11). The typical description of the local church in the New Testament stresses this sense of non-belonging. We are dealing with the church not of Pontus or of Galatia but with God's scattered people who lodge for a while in these places.

The working out of this being in the world yet not of it, avoiding on the one hand the lure of escape and on the other the peril of being assimilated, is the continuing struggle of Christians. The known difficulty of this narrow path will make us avoid simplistic judgements about our forefathers. We shall thus be wise to avoid the dogma of the original fall of Christianity in the era of Constantine and an understanding of the Church which would imagine that it could develop in a container hermetically sealed from society around it. The world rubs off on the Church and the Church, for good or ill, influences the world. In dealing with the particular situation of the Church of England it should not be imagined that an established church such as ours is alone in having a relationship with the state. As the 1970 Commission on Church and State insisted:

All churches have a basis in law. Their constitutions and rules are enforceable under the law relating to voluntary associations. Their property and endowments are held under trusts which are sometimes defined by reference to the doctrines and forms of worship of the church concerned.[1]

This blurring of the distinction between established and non-established churches helps us to read the history of the tension between church and state with honesty and sympathy. We are prepared to meet ecclesiastics who become politicians and politicians who become reformers of the church. It was for the love of Christ that Gregory the Great reluctantly emerged in the political arena and for the same love that Charles the Great reformed the church. Indeed, in the period following the conversion of Europe, the distinction between sacred and secular simply cannot be made. Kings were churchmen, crowned and anointed by the church, and ecclesiastics were often politicians as much as they were priests. When there was conflict it took place, not between the church and some antagonistic or even neutral body, but within the Christian community. It was within Christendom that the two great power blocks, papacy and monarchy, struggled for supremacy. In this struggle it is by no means clear that the clergy always represented the forces of light and princes those of darkness. Yet, despite tension and conflict, pope and monarch accepted one another within the Christian community. Princes might seek to clip the wings of the growing centralized power of Rome, and Rome might reply with the weapons of spiritual sanctions, but both knew that they had to live with one another. Despite the myth, which the sixteenth-century reformers tried to create, of a once independent national church, this was as true of England as of any other part of Europe. For all the conflict between Henry II and his archbishop, the *Ecclesia Anglicana* was conscious of being 'that portion of the Western Church which the Most High had planted in England'.[2]

To insist on seeing the relationship between church and nation in England against this wider background is not to ignore the particularity of that relationship created by the Reformation. The conflict of interest between pope and monarch was overcome by the simple expedient of denying any rights to the former.

The King's Majesty hath the chief power in this Realm

5

of England, and other his Dominions, unto whom the chief Government of all Estates of this Realm, whether they be Ecclesiastical or Civil, in all causes doth appertain, and is not, nor ought to be, subject to any foreign Jurisdiction . . . The Bishop of Rome hath no jurisdiction in this Realm of England.[3]

This was a resolution of the tension to which not even Henry II had aspired. The English Reformation was achieved by an act of nationalization. The Act of Supremacy of 1559 sought to restore the situation pioneered by Henry VIII but reversed by Mary. It was 'an act restoring to the crown the ancient jurisdiction over the state ecclesiastical and spiritual, and abolishing all foreign power repugnant to the same'. Office-holders in state and church were required to take the oath:

I — do utterly testify and declare in my conscience that the Queen's highness is the only supreme governor of this realm and of all other her highness' dominions and countries, as well in all spiritual or ecclesiastical things or causes as temporal, and that no foreign prince, person, prelate, state or potentate hath or ought to have any jurisdiction, power, superiority, preeminence or authority, ecclesiastical or spiritual, within this realm.[4]

From that time on the Englishman's allegiance was not to be divided between the claims of monarch and pope, for the realm was under a single head. The tone of the English Reformation was anti-clerical, not only in relation to the bishop of Rome but, as Elizabeth's ground-down bishops were to discover, in relation to all prelates. But this was not seen as the victory of the secular over the sacred; it was a victory of Christian laity over the priests. The prince in whose hands was gathered so much power was meant to be the 'godly prince'. As Paul Avis has written: 'The theory of the godly prince was not what it may appear to us to have been, an appeal from church to state in what was essentially a religious matter. It was an appeal from one officer to another within a single society, the Christian commonwealth.'[5]

Richard Hooker, the sixteenth-century apologist of the Elizabethan Settlement, gave the classic exposition of this relationship between church and state. It was not that the sweeping powers given to the monarch as supreme governor were absolute powers. Article 37 of the Church of England makes this clear: 'We give not to our Princes the ministering either of God's Word, or of the Sacraments.' Hooker goes further:

> We must note that their power is termed supremacy as being the highest, not simply without exception or anything. For what man is so brain sick as not to except in such speeches God himself, the King of all dominion? Who doubteth but that the King who received it, must hold it of, and under the law according to the old axiom 'The King assigns to the law that power which the law has assigned to him.' And again 'The King ought not to be under man but under God and the Law.'[6]

Royal supremacy is not a slipping back into a pagan divinizing of the state. The supreme governor is under God and under the law. Yet Hooker has no qualms about ecclesiastical matters being under laypersons, the Queen and Parliament. He is a child of the Reformation, unable to accept that 'freedom of the church' which, in the past, seemed to mean the freedom of the clergy.

> Till it be proved that some special law of Christ hath for ever annexed unto the clergy alone the power to make ecclesiastical laws, we are to hold it a thing most consonant with equity and reason that no ecclesiastical laws be made in a Christian commonwealth without consent as well of the laity as of the clergy, but least of all without the consent of the highest power.[7]

In Hooker's view not only is the role of the laity thus affirmed in the affairs of the state but the dignity and high vocation of the state is emphasized. The fact that Parliament deals with things spiritual shows the importance of government: 'The Parliament is a court not so merely temporal as if it might meddle with nothing but only leather and wool.'[8] 'A gross error it is to think that regal power ought to serve for the good of the body and not of the soul; for men's temporal peace and not for their eternal safety; as if God had ordained kings for no other end and purpose but only to fatten up men like hogs and to see that they have their mast.'[9] It was the achievement of the Reformation to rescue the church from being simply the clergy of the church and to give to the royal priesthood of the laity its rightful dignity. In doing this the New Testament's emphasis on the high calling of the state was recaptured. All concerns, whether sacred or secular, were related to the lordship of Christ. In this was permanent gain.

Yet the foundation upon which Hooker built his noble edifice was that all members of the nation were also members of the Church of England.

We hold that seeing there is not any man of the Church of England but the same is also a member of the commonwealth; nor any member of the commonwealth which is not also of the Church of England. Therefore, as in a figure triangle the base doth differ from the sides thereof, and yet one and the self same line is both a base and also a side; a side simply, a base if it chance to be the bottom and under lie the rest. So albeit properties and actions of one do cause the name of a commonwealth, qualities and functions of another sort, the name of a church to be given to a multitude; yet one and the self same multitude may in such sort be both.[10]

It is from this understanding of the identity of church and society that there flows the ability of princes to be involved in matters ecclesiastical. Only those, argues Hooker, who hold the contrary view 'that church and the commonwealth are two, both distinct and separate societies' can hold that 'the bishops may not meddle with the affairs of commonwealth . . . or kings with making laws for the church.'[11]

In this Hooker is in accord with most of his contemporaries who, whatever their religious differences, could not conceive of a society in which different religions could co-exist. The plank which crosses the deep Reformation divide is that of 'cuius regio, eius religio', there must be one religion under one monarch. Edwin Sandys, Archbishop of York under Elizabeth, thus expressed the view of Catholic and Protestant alike when he wrote:

> This liberty, that men may openly profess diversity of religion must needs be dangerous to the commonwealth. What stirs diversity of religion hath raised in nations and kingdoms the histories are so many and plain, and in our times insuch sort have told you, that with further proof I need not trouble your ears. One God, one King, one faith, one profession, is fit for one monarchy and commonwealth. Let conformity and unity in religion be provided for; and it shall be as a wall of defence unto this realm.[12]

But Hooker was too late; already the foundation stone of his theory, although buttressed by force of law, was being eroded by the tides of religious diversity. Not even Elizabeth's capacious bag, which held so many differences in belief and which required only that men fitted themselves into a framework of outward conformity, could contain the lively religious divergences of England. To the right were the recusants still hoping for a return to the old religion; to the left those who believed that the English Reformation was far from complete. In the judgement of Patrick McGrath in his *Papists and Puritans under Elizabeth I*:'The national church which was established by the Acts of Uniformity and Supremacy of 1559 was national only in the sense that all Elizabethans were required by law and under various penalties to adhere publicly to it and to attend its

9

services.'[13] So too Claire Cross has to conclude her study of the royal supremacy in the Elizabethan church with the view that 'as supreme governor over the English Church Elizabeth achieved only a partial success.'[14]

The pluralist society had arrived and the state was first to recognize its arrival. Driven, not so much by a passionate belief in the virtue of tolerance as by weariness with religious bigotry and strife, the eighteenth and early nineteenth centuries saw the nation coming to terms with reality. Dissenters were allowed first the freedom to worship in their own way and then full admittance into the national life; finally a similar freedom and acceptance were extended to those who had most appeared a threat to that national unity under the Crown, the Roman Catholics. It took a longer time for the church to recognize that the rock on which Hooker had built his theory had been eroded and to face the implications of this erosion.

Thomas Arnold, in his *Principles of Church Reform* (1833), showed how Hooker's theory might be reapplied in a liberal and reforming way. If the nation had ceased to adhere to the Church of England this was because the comprehensiveness of the Elizabethan settlement had not proved comprehensive enough. The solution lay in trying to widen its embrace. 'There is a choice', he argued, 'between entire agreement with a very few or general agreement with many.'[15] Believing that the latter course should be taken, he advocated a widening of the establishment. Although the church may be 'necessarily unable to command conviction on matters of opinion, it may yet lawfully regulate matters of practice.'[16]

> The real question is not what theoretical articles a man will or will not subscribe to, but what essential parts of Christian worship he is unable to use . . . The addressing Christ in the language of prayer and praise, is an essential part of Christian worship. Every Christian would feel his devotions incomplete if this formed no part of them. This, therefore, cannot be sacrificed, but we are by no means bound to enquire

whether all who pray to Christ entertain exactly the same idea of his nature. I believe that Arianism involves in it some very erroneous notions as to the object of religious worship; but if an Arian will join in our worship of Christ and will call him Lord and God, there is neither wisdom nor charity in insisting that he shall explain what he means by these terms, nor in questioning the strength and sincerity of his faith in his Saviour, because he makes too great a distinction between the divinity of the Father and that which he allows to be the attribute of the Son.[17]

Not worrying much that such words commit him to the strange notion of a sliding scale of divinity, Arnold would buoyantly brush aside such problems as 'mere theory'. For him the establishment had failed because it still had too many rough edges for dissenters; a lingering sacerdotalism and beliefs in apostolic succession needed to be smoothed down in order to create a truly national church. Arnold recognizes that such an establishment would fail to embrace Roman Catholics. He abhors the scurrilous language of popular anti-popery but admits that Catholic belief in the infallibility of the church, 'a fond effort of the human mind to believe in the reality of the support which its weakness so needed', and their adherence to the idea of a religious 'universal empire' would make it impossible for Roman Catholics to be comprehended in this wider establishment. Despite Arnold's sensitivity towards the needs of the new industrial areas and his imaginative proposals for institutional reform, his views rest on a dogmatic rejection of dogma.

Arnold accepts that the establishment is secure only on the foundation of the identification of church and nation. 'Religious society is only civil society enlightened; the state in its highest perfection becomes the church.' Along with Hooker, he does indeed believe that church and nation, 'are properly identified' and declares his allegiance to 'the noble, the divine theory that the Christian nation of England was the Church of England . . . the head of that

11

nation was for that very reason the head of the church, and every Englishman was supposed to be properly a member of it.'[18]

Arnold, with great honesty, does not evade the social implications of this theory. If a citizen rejects membership of the Church of England should this not lead to an exclusion from civil rights? The issue is faced and the results of this liberalizing of the establishment are seen to be what most would judge to be severely illiberal.

It is objected to this doctrine that it implies the exclusion of those who are not members of the church from the civil rights of citizens. I think it does imply such an exclusion in the case of those who are not members of the church of Christ; nor should I consider a Christian nation justified in forming a legislative union with a nation of Jews or Mahometans or Heathens. If the citizens of the same nation are in nearly equal proportions Christians and Heathens the state in that country is not yet sufficiently enlightened to become a church — and it is here that our Lord's words apply that 'his kingdom is not of this world': — Christians have no right as such to press the establishment of their religion to the prejudice of the civil rights of others. Yet if the two religions happened to be for the most part loosely divided, it would be a reason why such a nation should separate itself in two, and the Christian and Heathen portions of it form each a state distinct from the other. But when the decided majority of a country become Christians, so that the state may justly become a church, then the Heathen part of the population ought to be excluded from the legislature and encouraged, if it be possible, to emigrate to other countries, if they complain of not participating in the full rights of citizenship. At present in England I should earnestly deprecate the admission of the Jews to a share in the national legislature. It is a principle little warranted by authority or by reason, that the sole qualification for

12

enjoying the rights of citizenship should consist in being locally an inhabitant of any country.[19]

Such arguments have been heard more recently in debates on nationality and they have come from those who, like Arnold, are unwilling to accept a truly pluralist society. For all his ecclesiatical liberalism, Arnold ends up in some curiously illiberal company but, of course, this springs from the simple fact that he, like Elizabeth I before him, had to face the fact that even this capacious and comprehensive establishment had to have some limits.

A more theologically sensitive defence of the national church came from F.D. Maurice. He is firm in his adherence to those principles of the English Reformation which proclaimed a high doctrine of civil government and the value of the state to the church. A church entwined with the state enables us 'to rid ourselves of the Manichaean notion that the outward and visible universe and the ordinary social relations are the creations of an evil spirit to be esteemed lightly by all who have attained to the perception of a higher economy.'[20] Christians can never wash their hands of politics as being 'a dirty game' of which the spiritually minded should steer clear. Moreover, because the world, in the Johannine sense of human life organized against God, can infect the church as much as the state, it seemed to him clear:

from experience as well as reason, that the state is an excellent admonisher to the church respecting her inward corruptions, because it comes in contact with those outward evils which are the fruits of them, even as the church is a most excellent admonisher to the state respecting its sins, because their effects in destroying the nation's heart are most evident to the spiritual man.[21]

Maurice believed in national churches because he believed that the formation of national societies was part of God's great scheme. Indeed he held that the apostolic unestablished church was in a sense a church incomplete. 'We say

13

that this condition was necessarily imperfect, for it left all the relations of men, as held together by the bonds of neighbourhood, as distinguished by race and language, unaccounted for; for it did not bring these relations under church influence.'[22] This is why Maurice insists that a Christian doctrine of church and state must take with full seriousness the testimony of the Old Testament, for it is here that we learn, what is for him, that union of sacred and secular to which we should aspire. And yet Maurice cannot be said wholly to absorb the church in its national form. If the Old Testament bears witness to the state, the New Testament points us to the universal society. Against the Quakers, he has argued that there are certain permanent ordinances, Bible, creeds, sacraments, ministry 'in which the character and universality of the church are expressed'.[23]

There are two principles struggling within Christendom which Maurice would see reconciled:

the one, that which is embodied in Protestantism, resisting the claim of the spiritual power to any extra-national domination, and always tending to set at naught spiritual authority altogether; the other, that which is embodied in Romanism, resisting the attempts of the particular states to divide their own subjects from the rest of Christendom, continually striving to uphold the church as a separate power, and to set at naught the existence of each particular nation.[24]

Maurice brings to his support of the national church a much stronger sense of the particular roles of state and church. The state is to proclaim the law of God, the church the gospel. 'We believe that God has appointed one body, the state, as his minister for dealing with the outward formal, visible conduct of men, and another minister, the church, for dealing with the inward spiritual invisible origin of that conduct. Abolish the distinction, confound acts with principles, and of necessity you merge the one in the other.'[25]

Although Maurice seeks partnership between church and state, for him it is important that the integrity of their distinctive roles be maintained. Indeed it is by union and partnership, not by separation, that he sees this integrity best preserved: 'The church has become secular when she has attempted to realise herself as a separate body, the nation has become secular when it has tried to realise itself as a separate body. But each does so by violating the law of its existence, by refusing to be that which scriptures affirm and history proves that it was meant to be.'[26] Although his emphasis on the differing functions of church and state prepares him for a coming to terms with the fact of a pluralist society, it is partnership that he still seeks: 'A national church strong in the conviction of its own distinctive powers paying respectful homage to those of the state.'[27]

It was that respectful homage which the fathers of the Oxford Movement found impossible to pay. If, amidst the 'dreaming spires' they seemed so absorbed in magnifying the petty issues of university politics, that they failed to observe what was going on in the manufacturing cities of England, they none the less saw more clearly than others the fact of growing secularism, a nation falling away from all that was rugged and distinctive in Christian belief. The setting was mellow and soft but the foundations of faith which they had unearthed were as hard as rock. They saw the nation, whose representatives in Parliament controlled the affairs of the church, slipping away from that faith. The voice of the nation seemed to be that of Arnold, with his softening of the rock of dogma and apparent willingness to have the establishment embrace all who would conform, whatever their beliefs. How different was the picture of primitive Christianity which Hurrell Froude, a colleague of Newman's at Oriel College, had painted: a church free to affirm its own identity, free to choose those who were to be its spiritual leaders. The contrast between that 'ideal of a Christian church' and contemporary reality haunted a Balliol don, W.G. Ward:

Looking not at theories but at our own practical system in England, do we find anything even in the

15

remotest degree similar to this? A contemporary writer, who professes to be strictly in accordance with our divines of the 17th century pronounces at least his own opinion that 'the King has power, if he shall see cause, to suspend any Bishop for the execution of his office.' No single Bishop can so much as appoint the Ember Day prayer to be used on the week preceding his day for ordinations, should he see cause to change the latter. The only alterations, now ever made in our Prayer Book, are made by an Order of the Queen in Council.[28]

For Ward this longed-for independence and integrity did not mean simply a freedom in matters ecclesiastical; it involved a far less deferential demeanour towards the civil power. Although the church will not wish 'to draw into her hands the actual administration of state affairs . . . she will feel it her duty to proclaim aloud the general application of Christian principles to political government; and plain undeniable sins, such as a flagrantly unjust war, or a measure conspicuously oppressive to the poor, she will fearlessly denounce.'[29]

The call for independence came not only from the 'wild' ones like Froude and Ward. John Keble moved from the mild judgement that 'establishment is not on the whole as great a benefit to man's spiritual interest as we have been led to think' to sharper words:

We are the one religious body in the Queen's dominions to which the following privileges are expressly denied: To declare our own doctrines, to confirm, vary and repeal our own Canons, to have a voice in the nomination of our own chief pastors, to grant or withhold our own sacraments according to our own proper rules. If these disadvantages are inseparable from the position of our establishment then establishment must go.[30]

In fact Newman was to judge that the ideal 'or first

16

principle' of the movement 'was ecclesiastical liberty, the doctrine which it especially opposed was, in ecclesiastical language, the heresy of Erastus, and in political, the Royal Supremacy. The object of its attack was the Establishment, considered simply as such.'[31] Of course, by the time Newman made this judgement he was a Roman Catholic, and indeed it is the main burden of his lectures on *Certain Difficulties Felt by Anglicans* that the 'apostolical principles' of the movement were incompatible with the establishment. As he saw it, events had proved that the principles were a 'foreign substance' which the national church could not assimilate. Those who soldiered on in the Church of England, ever seeking to convert it to these principles, 'did not understand that the Established Religion was set up in Erastianism, that Erastianism was its essence, and that to destroy Erastianism was to destroy the Religion'.[32] To Newman it was clear, Erastianism, the ascendancy of the state over the church in ecclesiastical matters, had proved to be of the *esse* of the Church of England, so that if you looked for Catholic Christianity, you had to look elsewhere.

Others believed more firmly than Newman in the adaptive powers of the Church of England and events were to prove them right. Not all, but some, later disciples of the movement continued to see the reform of the church-state relationship as an outstanding item on its agenda. One of the sharpest minds was that of Father J.N. Figgis a monk of the Community of the Resurrection. He was no doctrinaire disestablishmentarian:

> What really concerns us is not so much whether or no a religious body be in a technical sense established, but whether or no it be conceived as possessing any living power of self-development, or whether it be conceived either as a creation of the state, or if allowed a private title is to be held rigidly under the trust deeds of her foundation, thereby enslaved to the dead . . . In other words, is the life of the society to be conceived as inherent or derived? Does the church exist by some inward living force, with powers of self-development

17

like a person; or is she a mere aggregate, a fortuitous concourse of ecclesiastical atoms, treated it may be as one for the purposes of convenience, but with no real claim to a mind or will of her own, except so far as the civil power sees good to invest her for the nonce with a fiction of unity?[33]

Although Figgis stood 'for Christianity as a distinct entity', he was more aware of the value of the pluralist society and of the need for positive Christian acceptance of such a society. He had a passionate concern for the battle for freedom in human society, in opposition 'to the notion of a single all-absorbing authority, the doctrine of the centrality of political power'. 'The battle of freedom in this century', he argued, 'is the battle of small societies to maintain their inherent life as against the all devouring Leviathan of the whole.' In fighting for the freedom of the church, 'we can claim that we are doing service no less valuable to the state than needful to the church.'[34]

The attack of Charles Gore, the Bishop of Oxford (1911–19), on establishment combined a touch of ecclesiastical rigorism with a passion for social justice. Established Christianity

whether in the civilised Roman Empire or in half-barbarous tribes or in modern nations, the sort of Christianity which claims to embrace the whole of society, which it costs nothing to profess and into which children are baptised practically as a matter of course, appears to be as audacious a departure from the method of Christ as can well be conceived.[35]

But, as Gore's writings and involvement in the Christian Socialist movement show, the freedom to be won for the church is not a selfish withdrawal from the world but gives the detachment necessary in its struggle against 'the substitution of economic man and his material interests for the complete man and his spiritual interests'.[36] This Christian service of society had to be performed with a full appreciation of the fact that the unity of church and society presupposed by the Middle Ages had now passed. Because there was no longer 'a common ecclesiastical authority presiding over the whole of human life,'[37] the reality of a pluralist society had to be faced.

Despite Newman's belief that apostolical principles could not be assimilated by the national church, in some measure they were. The Tractarian voice calling for the liberty of the church continued to be heard and in part acted upon. From the middle of the nineteenth century onwards the tide decisively turned in favour of the freedom of the Church of England. English pragmatism, nudged by church principle, led to a loosening of the bond between church and state. In practice, if not yet in theory, it became recognized that the foundation stone of establishment was beyond repair. A number of commissions bore witness to a nagging unease about the church-state relationship and the church was set on the path to self-government. From the resumption of debate in the Convocation of Canterbury in 1852, through the setting up of the Representative Church Council, combining both Convocations of Canterbury and York and the House of Laity in 1904 and its transformation into the Church Assembly in 1919, the movement was in one clear direction. The Synodical Government Measure of 1969, reconstituting representative systems in parish, rural deanery, diocese and at the national level by associating the House of Laity with the Convocations in all the work of the church, including worship and doctrine, was simply the climax of this movement. Zeal for self-government amongst churchmen joined hands with a growing distaste on the part of members of Parliament for dealing with church affairs, a distaste which grew after parliamentary rejection of the 1928 Prayer Book. When in 1964 Parliament was called upon to debate a measure concerning the clothing a clergyman should wear at divine worship, one speaker confessed to a feeling of almost indecent embarassment, and continued: 'that serves to underline the implicit plea which many have made tonight that the sooner the Church of England can be perfectly free to discuss these important matters and decide them for itself, the better it will be for the church and ourselves.'[38]

The Archbishops' Commission on Church and State (1970), chaired by Professor Owen Chadwick, can be seen as a response not only to the dissatisfaction of church members but to that parliamentary plea. The commission wisely turned its back on vague and emotive uses of the word 'establishment', such as its shorthand use for any in positions of authority or with reference to a conspiracy theory of a single power elite: 'For us "establishment" means the laws which apply to the Church of England and not to other churches.'[39] Thus it was quite definite and particular ties between church and state which were examined, and recommendations were made that church and state should stand rather further apart. The commission saw ecumenical and pastoral reasons why the development of self-government for the Church of England should take a significant step forward. It accordingly argued that the authority to order forms of worship already granted in part in the Prayer Book (Alternative and Other Services) Measure (1965) be granted finally to the General Synod and that this measure should also empower the synod to prescribe by canon the obligations of the clergy and certain lay officers to subscribe to the doctrine of the church and the forms of that subscription and also to interpret by canon the formularies of the church.

On the question of safeguards or limitations of the powers to be granted to the church, the commission was divided. Some members argued that the General Synod should in the last resort have power to authorize a new prayer book which would supersede that of 1662; others that such a proposal would be unacceptable to the church at large, to Parliament and possibly to the General Synod. They believed that powers to authorize forms of service which would be alternative to those of the 1662 book would be sufficient for the church.

The other main issue concerned the system for appointing bishops. The realities were nothing like so simple as appointment by the Crown on the advice of the prime minister, for widespread and, at points, formalized consultation had become part of the process; nevertheless there was dissatisfaction with the system. Again the commission, although united in recommending some change, gave divided counsel. Some believed in the modification of the existing system and a further formalization of the process of consultation. A church advisory committee would be set up which would be involved in the process of ascertaining candidates, shortlisting and nomination. Names would be put forward to the prime minister, but the Crown prerogative would remain untouched, for the prime minister would make the final choice and final submission to the Crown. Others held that to leave the prime minister to make the final choice was unacceptable. They argued for an electoral system in which the role of the prime minister would be eliminated. This group was confident that the flexibility of the British constitution was such that, were the Crown to be retained in the process, it could take in its stride the problem that the sovereign would have to act without the advice of a responsible minister. Although the commission made other recommendations, these on worship and doctrine and the appointment of bishops constituted its main plank.

The Commission, by thus attending austerely to particular laws which bound the Church of England to the state gave an impression of waving a wand and somewhat blandly conjuring away the privileged status of the established church which these laws created. Yet when pushed to say something about this status, as it had in the end reluctantly to be pushed, the commission declared itself for establishment. Although it protested that it was not blind to the pluralist nature of English society, it could not help but be attracted by the evidence of polsters who in 1968 had shown that some 50 per cent of the population still wanted to declare themselves members of the Church of England. Perhaps England was not as pluralist as it looked, and there remained enough of Hooker's foundation stone on which to lodge establishment:

We have not recommended a total severing of the historic links; first because we think such a proposal to be impracticable in the present state of opinion; and second because even if such a programme was practicable, most of us would not like it, though we should not shrink from it if the state decided it to be either wise or politically necessary.
The people of this country value various features of our polity, and will not favour too much tampering. The people of England still want to feel that religion has a place in the land to which they can turn on the too rare occasions when they think that they need it, and they are not likely to be pleased by legislation which might suggest that the English people as a whole were going unChristian.[40]

Since the beginning of the century, commissions on church and state have come and gone, and it is often said that, for all the talk, little has changed. The Chadwick Commission has had results; changes, albeit of a fairly conservative nature, have followed. On worship and doctrine the General Synod chose the more cautious approach, seeking only permanent powers to authorize services which would be alternative to those of the Book of Common Prayer. It was content that Parliament should remain custodian of the 1662 book. Yet even this mild measure did not pass through Parliament with quite the ease which was expected. Although the Worship and Doctrine Measure succeeded in the Commons by 145 votes to 45, the matter had raised more parliamentary concern than had been anticipated and there was substantial opposition to its passage. Mr Enoch Powell, in a speech of great lucidity, argued that the issue before the House was more fundamental than members realized. They were debating 'no less a question than the establishment of the Church of England itself — to be or not to be.' The characteristic shape of the English church derived from the fact that it is 'by law established'. The distinctive comprehensiveness of the church depended on the fact:

that its formulae and its liturgy, being established by the law of Parliament are peculiarly rigid and difficult of change. It was because the liturgy and the articles of religion, being part of the law of England, were so difficult to alter, were so near as possible permanencies, that in age after age successive waves of thought and religious feeling were nevertheless able to find a place within the Church of England and within its unity.

Mr Powell insisted that the only representatives of that Church of England were those who created the Church of England 'by establishing it by law, namely this House'.

The Church of England knows nothing of the Synod, but it is still the Church of England. There are still to be considered those millions of men and women to whom it belongs — albeit occasionally — and there are still those in generations yet to come for whom the comprehensiveness of the Church of England will give a religious home, a home in the church, which otherwise they would not find.[41]

On the question of the appointment of bishops, the General Synod in July 1974 passed a motion that 'the decisive voice in the appointment of diocesan bishops should be that of the church.' In passing this motion the Synod chose the more radical of the two paths indicated by the Chadwick Commission, despite a report of the standing committee which tried to fudge the issue by saying that in passing the motion the Synod would be committing itself to the proposition that 'ideally the Prime Minister will have no part in the effective process of selection and appointment.' Not unexpectedly, it proved that the Synod inhabited a less than 'ideal' world. Discussion with the party political leaders whittled down the Synod's aspiration, leaving it to come to terms with those more modest powers which the other members of the Chadwick Commission had advocated. The view of the politicians was that, as long as the Church of England remained by law established, the effective role of the prime minister could not be eliminated.

While the church could have a greater say, it could not have the decisive say; that must remain with 10 Downing Street. There was thus set up the Crown Appointments Commission, representing both the diocese in which the vacancy occurred and the wider Church of England. This would do far more than the vacancy in see committees which had been established to offer the Crown rather generalized comment on the needs of the diocese and the sort of candidate — saint, scholar or pastor — who was thought to be suitable. The Crown Appointments Commission was to go further. It was empowered to put up names to the prime minister in order of preference. The prime minister remains free to choose from that list or indeed to send it back to the Commission and ask for another list. It would however be a breach of the new agreement if the prime minister were to forward to the Crown a name which had not been on a Crown Appointments Commission list. The new procedure is a partnership between church and state, and the presence of the prime minister's appointments secretary as a non-voting member of the commission ensures that the views of the prime minister are represented throughout the process.

Although the new procedure cannot be said to have fulfilled the aspirations of the General Synod expressed in July 1974, it is certainly an advance along the road to self-government, and, it must be said, the Synod has settled back to enjoy the fruits of this new though limited freedom. Remarkably little curiosity has been shown about the workings of the Crown Appointments Commission. Indeed its proceedings have been so cloaked in a reverential veil of secrecy that it is difficult to see how an informed judgement can be made about it. Some authority, not the General Synod, has imposed upon members of the commission a solemn oath of silence. Although gossip and rumour run as swiftly and are savoured as deliciously in the corridors of Church House as in the Palace of Westminster, the church declares itself to be much enamoured of confidentiality.

There are clearly good reasons for such confidentiality but, as in other walks of public life, the cost of confidentiality is the loss of accountability. The commission has been insulated from informed criticism. We shall never know how satisfactory the new system is until we know also how many names the prime minister may have vetoed and on what grounds the veto has been exercised. If candidates are rejected, is it for doctrinal unorthodoxy or for political unsoundness or for what? These are apparently not the sort of questions the church wants to ask at present. It is sufficient that both in the appointment of bishops and in the control of worship and doctrine the church has advanced along the road to independence. Despite the warning signals sent out in the House of Commons debate on the Worship and Doctrine Measure and the rejection by the party political leaders of the church's aspiration to have the 'decisive' choice in the appointment of bishops which, taken together spelt out the message: 'as long as there is establishment, thus far and no further', the expectation of many churchmen in the 1970s was that there would be further developments in the direction of independence. We were set, it was believed, on the path of sure evolution to self-government.

In April 1981 this optimistic view received something of a shock when Parliament gave a second reading to the Prayer Book Protection Bill which required a parish church to use, on one Sunday in the month at the principal morning service, the Prayer Book of 1662 if this were requested by any twenty parishioners. Instead of bowing itself out of church matters, Parliament was intervening in the worshipping life of the Church of England at the most local level. It was only a gesture, for the matter was never forced home, but it was a significant gesture. The bill had arisen from the fear that the new Alternative Service Book, a child of Parliament's own Worship and Doctrine Measure, would in practice dislodge the Book of Common Prayer. Suddenly it was realized that, although in one way the 1662 Book was safe from the hands of the General Synod and defended by Parliament, in another way it was far from safe. The Prayer

Book might become like the old family Bible, greatly honoured but rarely used. A great fuss was generated and in a short time an extraordinary list of influential names was added to a petition protesting against the neglect of both the Prayer Book and the Authorized Version of the Bible. Many of the campaigners were devout Anglicans, some less so, but all were united in the belief that an act of cultural vandalism was taking place.

'DESTRUCTION of an INHERITANCE' shouted an advertisement placed in the newspapers by the McLaren Foundation. 'Is it really your wish that we and our future generations after us, shall now be deprived of the magnificent and accustomed prose of Cranmer's Prayer Book and the King James Bible, hammered out long ago in the white heat of a burning faith and a renaissance that raised the English language to a supremacy in the literature of Europe?' Along with wise comments made about the language of liturgy, to which the reformers should have paid careful attention, went wild and hysterical accusations of scheming and domineering clergymen who had deceived poor simple members of parochial church councils into bartering their Cranmerian birthright for a mess of modern liturgy. Visions were conjured up of thousands clamouring at the church door for their 1662 Prayer Book and being turned away deprived. Many a parson who faithfully celebrated the old rite Sunday by Sunday rubbed his eyes, looked ruefully at the empty pews, and wondered whether the protest would not have been more effective if the protesters had taken to their knees rather than to petitions and the correspondence columns of *The Times*. The thousands voting with their knees and thus packing their parish churches would surely have shaken the confidence of the promoters of modern liturgy. But the campaigners thought otherwise; to Parliament they went with their Prayer Book Protection Bill.

We cannot delay here over the pros and cons of Cranmerian liturgy. As one who is vicar of the church in which Thomas Cranmer was tried and condemned, I have more than a little respect for the power of his liturgy. Day by day I say morning and evening prayer from his book and on Sundays two out of the three main services in this church are conducted according to the 1662 rite. The Prayer Book Holy Communion service was celebrated more often in 1982 than it was in 1782. But it is with the implications for the church's relationship with the state that we are concerned here. During the debate on the Prayer Book Protection Bill, members of both houses rose to rebuke the national church. Parliament had no hesitation in affirming its right and duty to speak out on behalf of the members of the church above the strident tones of a narrow elite in the Synod, who represented no more than a thin line of active church-goers. 'The Synod,' cried the McLaren Foundation advertisement,

> now maintains that the change facilitates also certain proposed doctrinal amendments, but as a nation we have never attached much significance to man-made doctrine. One hundred Christians at a Church of England service might well hold almost as many minor variants of their belief and therein lies the Church's strength. It seems unlikely that they want the Synod's view on minor points of doctrine thrust down their throats and to pay moreover so high a price for it.

The words are those of the McLaren Foundation, but the sentiments are pure Arnold. The nation was rebuking the church for sectarian dogmatism. Something of this spilled over into the Palace of Westminster, where we saw renewed the conviction that the members of the Church of England are the members of the nation and thus Parliament is the true source of authority in the church's life. In a fit of absent-mindedness, during which only Mr Enoch Powell was awake, Parliament had handed to the Synod a limited freedom. Parliament had given an inch and greedy ecclesiastics had snatched a mile. The time had come for the Synod to be called to heel, to be reminded that as long as the church was established, it had a lord and master. 'The Church cannot have it both ways,' argued Lord Glenamara.

Either the Church of England retains its privileges of establishment and if so Parliament retains the right to intervene or Parliament surrenders that right and the Church of England surrenders its privileges. In the past the Church of England has tried, I think, rather to have the best of both worlds. The Worship and Doctrine Measure was followed by the new procedure for the Nomination of Bishops. These I think we saw many of us as two steps towards the disestablishment of the Church. But at the same time the Church holds up its hands in horror at any suggestion that this Sovereign Parliament should still have the right to legislate on Church matters except at the request of the Synod.[42]

That seemed fair comment, and it was underlined by others, including Lord Dacre of Glanton. He argued that the church authorities had broken 'the express terms of the autonomy conditionally granted to them', and claimed that they were seeking 'to change what has been called the life-blood of the Church. Had they stated openly that this was their intention, would Parliament have granted their autonomy? I do not think so. But they have adopted what is known as 'salami tactics' and now it is they who are effectively disturbing the agreed balance between church and state, and Parliament, I submit, has the duty in such cases to intervene to protect that balance.'[43]

While moderate church reformers in the 1960s and 1970s might have thought establishment to be a 'dead issue' and hoped for a fairly speedy withering away of the state connection, Parliament continues to think otherwise. For the state, establishment remains a complex package of privileges and restrictions, so that, as long as the Church of England remains established, it cannot have the former without enduring the latter. After that Parliamentary debate in 1981, there followed in the summer of 1982 a curious bundle of events which again brought the performance of the national church under public scrutiny. First the Church of England declined to turn the service commemorating the Falkland Islands campaign into an occasion of nationalistic triumphalism and insisted that an act of Christian worship should remain recognizably Christian. Then a new hymn book was announced which was going to amend certain verses in the National Anthem in a more pacific direction. Finally a working party of the Board for Social Responsibility produced a report on *The Church and the Bomb* which advocated unilateral nuclear disarmament. These three little episodes created a somewhat synthetic explosion of anger against the national church. Suddenly the church seemed to be full of Trotskyites and pacifists. One newspaper even called for its disestablishment. Most of this was an attempt either to keep alive the flagging 'Falklands' Spirit' or simply to entertain the public during the summer months, but added to the Prayer Book controversy, trivial though it was, it had the effect of unearthing a view about the relationship of church and nation which had always been present but dangerously ignored by churchmen in the 1960s and 1970s. There came a moment when the General Synod was discussing matters of church and state when the late Bishop Ronald Williams ruefully admitted that 'the tide of world history is running in the direction of disestablishment.' He then continued, with a glint in his eye (for he was a convinced believer in establishment): 'Of course tides can be reversed. When Archbishop Laud's head rolled in Whitehall one might have thought that the tide of history was running against episcopacy — but the bishops came back!'

The evolution of independence for the Church of England has received a setback. It may be that the tide is moving once again in the direction of establishment. Indeed it would not be surprising if the nation at a time of fragmentation were to rediscover the national church as a pot of glue which could assist in the holding together of society. It might thus prove that the Chadwick Commission was altogether too bland in its treatment of the special status of the established church. If this be the case, then Mr Enoch Powell's question 'to be or not to be', the question of establishment or disestablishment, rises again as a live issue.

2 Establishment — Good for the Church?

In the debate on the Prayer Book Protection Bill the Bishop of Durham defended the church. He was clear that establishment should stay. Indeed his argument was that unless Parliament accepted reasonable modifications in the church–state relationship, there would arise a clamour for disestablishment, and that was something he did not wish to see:

> We know that it would be a serious departure from established practice if Parliament were to break the tradition of over sixty years and try to impose legislation on the Church of England without consultation and against what I believe would be fierce opposition. There has been in the press and other places recently some sabre rattling on the subject of disestablishment. Let me declare myself. I am a firm believer in establishment. It would be a tragedy to further weaken the links between church and state. I believe it would be bad for the church because it would strengthen the sectarian elements within the church, and bad for the nation because now, at all times, we need in our nation some continuing corporate acknowledgement of religious beliefs and sanctions to give us direction.[44]

The Bishop of Durham articulates the belief of many that the continuing bond between church and state benefits both church and nation, so much so that to destroy it would be nothing less than a 'tragedy'. There are others like the bishop, worthy of respect, who hold this strong view. Let us then first examine in what way establishment may be good for the church.

As we have seen, there emerged from the English Reformation a strong belief that the government of the church should not be an exclusively clerical preserve. The rights of the laity were rediscovered. It was thus natural that the Sovereign in Parliament should bear rule in matters sacred as well as secular. Of course the assumption was that the prince should be the 'godly prince' and members of Parliament communicant members of the Church of England. Indeed by law this had to be. But circumstances changed. It had to be faced that a religiously pluralist society could only be represented by a religiously pluralist Parliament, and so the question was asked whether such an assembly, made up of people of many beliefs and none, could fittingly be the custodian of the worship and doctrine of the church. Yet when from the middle of the nineteenth century the church acquired organs of self-government, this was by no means a return to that clericalism which the old notion of the 'freedom of the church' had so often meant. The course of development was loyal to the insights of the Reformation; 'more loyal', most Presbyterians and Free Churchman would say. Through parochial church councils, diocesan conferences and the Church Assembly, the Church of England became accustomed to clergy and laity discussing matters of concern together. The idea that it was always the parson who dominated these councils brings a wry smile to the faces of those who have known the workings of church democracy in those remaining squire-ruled villages. With synodical government there was created a structure of decision-making which stretched from the parish to Westminster, and in which matters doctrinal and liturgical, as well as administrative and financial, were discussed by clergy and laity as partners.

The sound principle that lay sanity can help to clear the muddy waters of ecclesiastical politics is embodied more nearly in the synods of the church than in the Houses of Parliament. If Parliament now believes that the church is

31

failing to serve the nation and that its synods should be called to heel, it must be respectfully requested to meditate on the fact that it was Parliament which set up the church's structure of government and which devolved responsibilities to it. The Synod is a young body and it is not likely that its development into maturity will be assisted by Parliamentary intervention. On the whole children grow up best when they are allowed to let go of nurse and make their own mistakes. Nobody who has participated in synodical government can be unaware of its deficiencies. In fact one of its greatest is the inability to put a sufficient distance between itself and the Palace of Westminster. The shadow of its illustrious neighbour seems to encourage members of Synod to play at being members of Parliament and to indulge in a confrontation form of politics, appropriate enough in a body which contains not only Her Majesty's Government but also the official Opposition, but ill suited to an assembly which should be seeking, beyond the pressures of various factions, what is the truth of God.

In fact, when the Synod is confronted by some necessary theological issue, it is ill at ease, and time is not given for leisured theological reflection. There is a restlessness for movement back to the safer waters of pragmatism and ecclesiastical politics. Recent attempts to move towards Christian unity have shown that the pressures of hustling managers and the sepulchral cry 'Divide' have been less than helpful. In such matters more than majorities, whether of two-thirds or three-quarters, should be sought. Consensus is what a Christian assembly should be after. Here perhaps we have less to learn from Parliament and more from the Quakers who, in quite large assemblies, labour, not without success, to come to a common mind. The Synod has yet to discover a distinctive style of Christian discussion and decision-making. One is tempted to think that this would come more quickly if Church House were transported away from Westminster to Bootle or Hartlepool. Assuredly the Synod is not beyond criticism, yet in the end it shares the deficiencies common to all representative assemblies. It might indeed seem more self-critical than a

Parliament which consistently refuses to improve its representative nature by introducing a more equitable electoral system. When members of Parliament complain of the 'unrepresentative' nature of the Synod, one is inclined to say, with of course the deepest respect, 'Physician, heal thyself.'

The Bishop of Durham marshals another argument in favour of establishment. It is alleged to be good for the church because it counters the forces of sectarianism. Thus it is believed that its links with the state ease the church out of a ghetto existence and force it to be an open church. We recall Mr Enoch Powell's argument that Parliament in providing a framework for the church 'particularly rigid and difficult of change' offers a spiritual home for many who otherwise would not have one. The Church of England is thus forced to keep its doors open to the aspirations of folk religion and the tentative allegiance of uncommitted Christian fellow-travellers. The national church is a tolerant church, allowing seekers plenty of space to make their own way into the faith and scholars freedom to question even the fundamentals of that faith. This inheritance of liberality, although often uncomfortable to live with, rests not on an indifference to faith but on a confidence that the God of truth can be trusted to maintain his church in truth. It is a conviction of the Church of England that the dangers of such liberality are less than those of rigorism and heresy hunting. The writer finds himself convinced of the value of this inheritance. Indeed, in his memorandum of dissent to the main findings of the Chadwick Commission he wrote: 'I am utterly committed both by theological conviction and pastoral experience to the view that the church should be involved in the life of the nation and should retain its historic liberality and openness.'[45]

It is often said that the Church of England must choose between being the established church or being a sect. In this we encounter the slipperiness of the noun 'sect' and its adjective 'sectarian'. Dictionary definitions of 'sect' usually refer to 'a body of people who unite in holding some particular views', although often it carries the implication that the view held is a minority dissenting view swimming against the tide of main-stream opinion. In this sober descriptive sense it would be hard to describe any church in a pluralist society as other than a 'sect'. All churches have particular views and usually they are minority views. Thus Karl Rahner the Jesuit theologian can write that the church in the present situation, which he calls that of the 'diaspora', has 'sociologically speaking the character of a sect in contrast to that of a church of the vast mass of people, a church in possession'.[46] In such a situation 'Christianity ceases to be a religion of growth and becomes a religion of choice'; the church 'if it is to remain alive at all will be a church of active members, a church of the laity', while the clergy are 'deprived of status in the sociological sense'. Most Christians can recognize the contemporary situation of the church in that description. In this sense of the word 'sect' the Methodist, Baptist, Roman Catholic and United Reformed churches would be seen as sects, and so too surely would be the Church of England, which is sociologically in precisely the same boat. There is really no question of choosing about it; we, along with other Christians, have had this thrust upon us by a pluralist society. However at this point a further nuance is introduced into the word 'sect'. It is imported from the adjective 'sectarian' which, in its dictionary definition, carries the implication that the identity of the sect leads to narrowness and bigotry. 'Bigotedly devoted to the interests of a sect, narrow, exclusive' is how one dictionary defines 'sectarian'.

In claiming that the choice before the Church of England is between being the national established church and being a sect, this secondary and more emotive definition has been smuggled in and the suggestion conveyed that, in order to be open and unbigoted, the church must choose the former. Involved in this muddle over the word 'sect' is the distressing implication that all the other great churches of Christendom, apart from the very few which are established, are mere sects, and that national established churches have some monopoly of liberality and openness. Knowing that this is not the case, it becomes evident that these virtues flow from sources other than the status of establishment.

There are those who might be unhappy with the description of the Church of England as 'a body of men who unite in holding some particular views'. 'That,' they might say, 'is precisely what the national church is not. While the sect or denomination finds its unity in common belief, the bonds which bind the members of the national church together are those of an institutional framework and a fixed liturgy.' It is this view which often underlies the agitation about the Book of Common Prayer and why some critics of the Synod reject its claim to represent the Church of England. While the Synod may fairly be said to represent those ecclesiastical 'activists' who have a number of 'particular views', only Parliament can be trusted to represent that silent majority which is content to accept the liturgy and institutions of the national church. 'Who,' asked Lord Dacre,

> are the advocates of these [liturgical] innovations? . . .
> They are not the Church. The Church is the congregation of the faithful, clergy and laity alike, and it includes many who loyally adhere without pedantically subscribing. That is the difference between a Church and a sect. An established church has a particular duty of tolerance and comprehension. The laity is not to be dragged unwillingly forward along a particular road by a party of activists exploiting their customary loyalty and deference.[47]

It would be interesting to know how the noble lord would define 'the congregation of the faithful' and distinguish between those 'loyally adhering' and those 'pedantically subscribing'. How faithful should the faithful be and what, in practice, constitutes loyal adherence? Yet, from these somewhat misty words there emerges a recognizable understanding of the Church of England. It is less a community to be joined than an institution whose officers provide certain services which the nation has a right to expect when

35

it calls for them. Thus, when the nation, after the Falkland Islands conflict, called for a victory service, the national church should have provided it. At a deeper level such a church is believed to provide a framework of liturgy and ceremony which upholds the individual as he makes his own way to God and works out his own beliefs. Belief is not the bond which binds members of the church together but a private matter, 'between myself and God', which yet requires a minimum of social religion to sustain it. Although there is an echo here of the Elizabethan settlement, it is in truth a rather faint echo, for, in its modern form, it is considerably more lax in its demand for conformity. As the lord chancellor reminded his fellow peers, the Act of Uniformity of Elizabeth I carried a fine of four hundred marks for those who did not attend their parish church on a Sunday,[48] and, although it was only a few persons who had to subscribe to the Thirty-Nine Articles, there was for the laity the catechism to be learned. 'All fathers, mothers, masters and dames, shall cause their children, servants and prentices (which have not learned their Catechism) to come to the church at the time appointed, and obediently to hear, and be ordered by the Curate, until such time as they have learned all that is here appointed for them to learn' (Book of Common Prayer, rubric attached to A Catechism). For the church of Elizabeth I, loyal adherence involved both church-going and the sharing of a common faith. The liberal establishment of Thomas Arnold and Lord Dacre is a somewhat watered-down version.

Yet here is an understanding of the Church of England which is far from dead; by ignoring it and failing to engage with it we have allowed the Prayer Book debate to become the bad-tempered and fruitless thing it has been. The debate forces us to trace our differences back to different understandings of the church which are, in turn, based on different understandings of the nature of the Christian enterprise. In truth it reaches down to the fundamental issue as to whether Christianity is built on the religious aspirations and search of men or on the movement of God towards us in self-disclosure. As we shall see later the 'pilgrim' or 'search' image is valuable in our understanding of the conditions necessary for individuals to grow in faith, but here we must first affirm that the church is a society fashioned and shaped by the revelation of God. We nail our colours to the mast: the central insight of our faith is the perception of God's gracious movement towards us, of the mystery once hidden now disclosed, of the God who has spoken in fragmentary and varied fashion through the prophets, now speaking in his Son. The Christian heart of the matter is that out of silence God has spoken and his word has been made flesh in Jesus. What stands before the believer is not a changeless institution or liturgy — the institutions of Christianity have proved remarkably flexible and the history of liturgy is a history of change, one of the more startling of which changes was Cranmer's Prayer Book. The unchanging rock is Jesus Christ the same yesterday, today and for ever. Confronted by God's self-disclosure, I am no longer left to my poor intellectual and spiritual resources. It is this fundamental insight which the Oxford fathers so passionately defended when they affirmed dogma and opposed theological liberalism. In the view of liberalism, wrote Newman,

> Revealed religion is not a truth, but a sentiment and a taste; not an objective fact, not miraculous; and it is the right of each individual to make it say just what strikes his fancy. Devotion is not necessarily founded on faith. Men may go to Protestant Churches and to Catholic, may get good from both and belong to neither. They may fraternise together in spiritual thoughts and feelings, without having any views at all of doctrines in common, or seeing the need of them.[49]

The church must be built, not on these shifting sands of human opinion, but on the rock of God's revelation.

The identity of the church is shaped by its apostolicity, so that as the Son was sent by the Father, the apostles are sent out by the Son. This establishing of the church's identity is not a once-for-all event as if it poured off the apostolic production line complete and unchanging. This is a community which moves through a real and therefore changing world but, in and amongst the changes, it seeks again and again to renew its identity by resisting the temptation to be conformed to every passing fashion and by attending anew in each unique situation to the Word of God in Jesus. The church can never be at home in any culture, it is permanently in exile, its life hid with Christ in God, sharing his heavenly citizenship. This detachment of the church does not spring from a selfish desire to cultivate its own soul or to pretend that it is the only oasis of light in a dark world but from its absolute obligation to hear the Word of God, who is truth, and to have its worship, faith and order shaped by him. Thus no authority or assembly should have the right to control the church's life which does not deliberately and consciously seek to be the servant of that Word.

By insisting on its freedom to be itself, the church strikes a blow against the claims of the monopolistic state and of idolatrous nationalism. As Father Figgis showed, this refusal to allow all power and authority to flow from one source assists the growth of a liberal pluralist society. Indeed it is strange that conservatives anxious to 'roll back the frontiers of the state' do not apply this principle to the Church of England. If one is concerned to decentralize and disperse power, the church would surely be a good candidate for 'privatization'. It is probably a just claim that the English Reformers, by breaking with Rome, assisted in the breaking of a too uniform imperialist Christianity. The ideal of an independent national church certainly helped the growth of Christian variety and pluralism, yet, by gathering all causes ecclesiastical as well as temporal under the Crown, a dangerous subservience to the state was fashioned. If the local church had more freedom to fashion its distinctive life, in breaking with the papacy the international dimension of Christianity was threatened, leaving the church in unhealthy isolation and at greater risk of becoming a captive of the developing class structure.

If the church is shaped by the gift and call of God then it is less an institution existing to provide religious ceremonies for the nation than a community which has to be joined. No one has a right, by virtue of being English, to be a member of it. No one is born into the church. The only way into the church is that which has existed from earliest times — to receive the gift of God given in baptism and to make a free personal response to that gift. Grace and faith, not nationality, form the only gateway into the church. If there is no Christianity without the gift of God equally there can be no discipleship without decision and commitment. What God seeks is simply our 'Yes' to his loving approach so that, although friends can carry me into the presence of the Lord and lay me at his feet, ultimately no one can say 'Yes' to God for me.

Just because there is so much that is good about the tolerance and openness of the Church of England, it is important that we do not distort it into a sentimental indulgence. To give the appearance that the gift of the gospel can be had without obligation and duty is to foster a cruel illusion and a parody of love. Anybody who knows anything about human love knows that love without demand, far from being creative, is destructive. Of course the church must be kept open to all human searching for God, whether it be the first faltering steps of those finding the way out of a narrowly secularist world or the barely articulate aspiration in what is called 'folk religion'. All reaching out towards God must be able to find its home and fulfilment within the church. But this does not mean that these first steps or aspirations can be identified with the Christian faith. Certainly it is not the case that every person who describes himself to an enquiring pollster as a Christian is thereby a Christian, for being a Christian is more than a self-description whose meaning each individual can invent. I may describe myself as a member of a political party but unless I have paid my dues the local party secretary may challenge this self-description. Indeed when people casually describe themselves as Christian or C of E, it is notoriously difficult to discover what they mean by it.

Pollsters seem to find that it is thought compatible with 'being C of E' neither to share its beliefs nor to practise its morals nor to take part in its prayer and worship. Being a Christian may simply mean being a good person — though not too good, for that would be hypocrisy and no Englishman would like to be accused of that.

This is not a remote issue. Parish priests daily confront situations which embody it. Shall I baptize the infant of parents who will not even avail themselves of the opportunity of discovering what they are asking for? Should I, without question, 'church' the mother who comes to me saying that she cannot enter a neighbour's house without this 'cleansing'? What shall I do about the demand of two parishioners to be married in the parish church who, having every legal right to be married there, yet tell me explicitly that they have repudiated their baptism and are atheists but come to the parish church because the decor in the local registry office is so depressing? These are no wild clerical nightmares but real cases I have known. Of course there are some rigorists whose fingers itch to plaster every ordinance of the church with warning signs, with rules and regulations. But most of us are not like that; we are rather worried pastors who want to say 'yes', who are adept in giving the benefit of the doubt, who try to be both loving and honest. We want to say 'yes'; it is easier to say 'yes'; but in our heart of hearts we know that true pastoral love requires discrimination. In truth the 'folk religion' we encounter is a complex and ambiguous phenomenon for, woven around a scarcely recognized longing for faith, are often notions of God which range from the sentimental to the disastrous and include a good measure of pure nostalgia. No responsible pastor, who wants to blow upon the smoking flax and see it ignite into strong faith, can simply accept the package with a benign indifference to its darker contents. The door of the church is to be an open door but not to open like the door of a stage set on to nothing. There stands before the one who enters the rock of God's reality revealed in the dying and rising of the Lord Jesus by whom all our religion, whether folk or otherwise, is judged.

What God offers is not just a place in a club which welcomes non-playing as well as playing members, but the awful seriousness of becoming a member of the body of his Son Jesus Christ. Before each one of us there stands the Word of God which is sharper than any two-edged sword. When the Chadwick Commission said that it believed that the people of England 'are not likely to be pleased by legislation which might suggest that the English people as a whole were going unChristian', it failed to see that the issue is not what might please the people of England but what is the fact of the matter. 'Love grows by means of truth', said Pope John Paul II at Canterbury, which suggests that, although it might not be the most popular thing, to face the fact that kindly English people have advanced a good way down the road from recognizably Christian beliefs and values might be the most loving thing.

God has spoken in the Word made flesh and he has sent his church to bear witness to that Word. That is what gives the church its distinctive, set-apart identity. But with this has to be a positive openness. There is something in the genial tolerant life of the Church of England to be cherished and wedded to that rock-like Christian affirmation which the fathers of the Oxford Movement called 'dogma'. Amongst the heroes of this Anglican openness are many parish priests who have been content to immerse themselves in the life of a particular locality. They have cared for the congregation of the faithful, the little flock of Christ, knowing that it had an undeserved vocation to proclaim the wonderful deeds of him who has called us out of darkness and to be, in that place, the body of Christ, expressing in flesh and blood his living presence. And yet the care of such priests has extended way beyond the congregation to embrace all who lived in that area and all its concerns. They have made the small Christian community look out from itself to be fascinated by and care for the quality of life in the parish, its homelife, its leisure, its work and its politics. In such ministries, without a lot of talk or self-advertisement, the truly catholic vocation of the church is fulfilled. People go out from a firm sacramental centre not into the devil's world but into God's world, alerted to discern in every place the same Lord who has made himself known in the breaking of the bread. Here as Newman said is the Church of God 'on visitation through the earth, surveying, judging, sifting, selecting, and refining all matters of thought and practice; detecting what was precious amid what is ruined and refuse, and putting her seal upon it'.[50]

It is not the spirit of openness which the disestablishmentarian challenges but the argument that it depends upon the particular laws which bind the Church of England to the state. Of course structures and institutions can assist or hinder this spirit, but it is a matter of observation that, while some clergy of the establishment can be rigorist and exclusive, other clergy of non-established churches admirably purvey it. All of us have known a similar fascination with the world and a similar pastoral gentleness and sensitivity amongst our Free Church and Roman Catholic brethren. The established church has in truth no monopoly of the spirit of openness. If we are in search of structures which buttress this spirit then it is to the parochial system we should look. This provides the parson with a given area, encourages him to lift his sights beyond the claims of the Christian congregation and makes him open to the needs of all comers. A parochial system, as anyone who knows the Church in Wales recognizes, can be retained in a disestablished church. In the judgement of some who know that church, once it had been stripped of its established status, which gave it the appearance of an alien intruder, it has become more truly a people's church, a national church capable of providing a home for the religious aspirations of many.

In truth the roots of such openness strike deeper than the establishment. They rest in the soil of the gospel demand that the church be catholic as well as holy. This involves the church in the peculiarly difficult task of establishing its identity while being radically open to the world. The temptation is to seek a holiness or identity which is not that of Christ. His is a catholic holiness, a holiness of love which boldly risks itself by breaking through the barriers of ritual uncleanness and welcoming all to himself. He is the one who eats with tax-gatherers and sinners and, in so doing, lays himself open to criticism by those who have chosen an elitist form of holiness. So, while pushing the claims of God to their furthest extreme — 'You must be perfect, as your heavenly Father is perfect', he yet will not quench the smoking flax. By drawing near to us in our need and unsatisfactoriness, Jesus is the embodiment or sacrament of the accessible and therefore vulnerable God. It is God who in Christ risks his holiness for the sake of love and who calls the Christian community, as the body of that Christ, to be the continuing sign of this holy love. In the church's sacraments, preaching, pastoral care and common life, the vulnerable love of the living Jesus continues to be made tangible. Indeed the history of the church is that of the challenge to ever wider catholicity, to reach out beyond the confines of Judaism to the gentile world, to embrace new ways of thought, new cultures, to claim for Christ all things human, good and true. It is a risky enterprise, for all too easily can the world absorb the church into itself, and it is little wonder that the purists fear that the pearl of precious price will be trampled by swine; yet, despite the warning calls of those who would summon the church back into the safety of an exclusive and stagnant pool, the main stream sweeps on to take the risk and overflow its banks. Wheat and weeds must be allowed to grow together until the Lord's harvest. Judge nothing before the time.

There is no doubt that the church is again threatened by a purist rigorism, but the threat does not come from ministers struggling to do justice to the demand of love, nor from those who would affirm the integrity of the church's life; rather does it come from a worldly fear. Threatened by violence, war and recession, man is losing confidence in his ability to order the world in justice and peace. Things seem out of control, the problems so vast and complex that there is an almost irresistible temptation to opt out. Sects and bizarre cults, with their simplistic understandings of the world and their magical answers, have acquired a new appeal. Modern man, far from being the hard-headed confident secularist we once imagined him to be, seems to be a gullible prey to any superstitious nonsense. Christians have not been able to insulate themselves from this fear and from this mood of escapism. A nostalgic conservatism has once more become fashionable. Those who complain of 'trendy' radical clergymen are behind the times, for the new 'trendy' is more likely to be your short-back-and-sides young man who, in his sports jacket and flannels, thanks God that he is realist in politics, distrusts the activity of the mind in religion and sinks easily into some definite form of churchmanship. If this is what the Bishop of Durham fears, we fear it with him, and we are troubled when we see the heirs of the Oxford Movement clambering onto this bandwagon of emotional security. It is pitiful that the thought of so-called liberal theologians is met, not by deeper and more rigorous thought, but by cheap sneers and a retreat back into authoritarian forms of religion. Far from displaying a trust in God, such nervous steadying of the ark exposes our lack of confidence in his ability to maintain his own truth. But, of course, this new conservatism is just a passing fashion, as much influenced by its secular setting and therefore as 'trendy' as the wildest radical flights of the 1960s. It is wise to attend to the words of F.D. Maurice when he perceived the folly of 'opposing the spirit of the age with the spirit of a former age'.

If we take such sectarianism with the seriousness with which we take any disease, then we shall realize that there lies no cure in neo-establishmentarianism, which is simply another form of such escapism. A disease so old and deep-rooted can be cured only by a more profound under-standing of the gospel which is to shape the life of the church. Here we find the resources which enable us to marry the demands of Christian identity to those of openness. Instead of peering suspiciously from the ark of salvation into the world, we are encouraged to look at that world with a deeper hope. The Second Vatican Council spoke of:

the world as the theatre of human history, bearing the

marks of travail, its triumphs and failures, the world which in the Christian Vision has been created and is sustained by the love of its maker, which has been freed from the slavery of sin by Christ, who was crucified and rose again in order to break the stranglehold of the evil one, so that it might be fashioned anew according to God's design and brought to its fulfilment.[51]

Karl Rahner has spoken of a new 'optimism with regard to salvation' and described it as 'one of the most astonishing phenomena in the development of the Church's conscious awareness of her faith,'[52] while Anglicans will see a precursor of it in the insistence of F.D. Maurice that the world has Christ, not the devil, as its king. 'No man has a right to say My race is a sinful fallen race even when he most confesses the greatness of his own sin and fall, because he is bound to contemplate his race in the Son of God and to claim by faith in him his share in its redemption and glory.'[53]

This more optimistic way of looking at the world is reflected in liturgical and pastoral practice. The 1662 service for the Public Baptism of Infants begins with the words 'Forasmuch as all men are conceived and born in sin', and reflects the urgent need to rescue the unbaptized child from such sin in the rubric instructing the curates of every parish to 'admonish the people that they defer not the baptism of their children longer than the first or second Sunday after their birth'. Now there is no longer the same fear about the fate of the unbaptized and, as a consequence, not the same eagerness for early baptism. Of course, this is sometimes represented as a falling away from a belief in the reality of original sin. This is not the case. Although the understanding of such sin as a quasi-physical contagion has been implicitly rejected, the insight that we are born, not into a morally neutral vacuum, but into a bent world whose self-seeking rubs off onto us, is retained and indeed strengthened. With the new optimism goes a deeper sensitivity to the tragedy of the world, to our entanglement in the structures of sin: the good that we would, that we cannot do (Romans 7:19). We do not in truth slide smoothly into the kingdom of God but, in such a fix, cry out for redemption: 'Wretched man that I am, who will deliver me from this body of death?' (Romans 7:24) Any cheerful religion which preaches Christ risen but not crucified, any liturgy robbed of the tears of the Agnus Dei fails to make contact with real human need. And yet it is heresy, not orthodoxy, to hold that the deepest reality of the world is evil. The fall does not cancel out the creation. Over this world we are to exclaim with the creator: 'Behold, it is very good.' That cry does not come from superficial optimists who, amidst dancing daffodils, are able to view the world as benign and friendly, but from those who have tasted evil and destructiveness and are yet able to see beyond the darkness to the creating hands of God. Let us be sure about this, our faith rejects not only the pessimism which sees the world as fundamentally evil but also a dualism which sees the conflict between good and evil as an eternal conflict. While the mythology of the devil teaches us to take evil seriously, it is important to recall that the fierceness of the devil 'going about seeking whom he may devour' is that of a mortally wounded animal. The fundamental reality of created goodness, a non-dualistic understanding of the devil, these themes of orthodoxy need to be reaffirmed at a time when a world, which seems out of control, tempts us to a dark fatalism and a morbid fascination with the works of Satan.

This vision of the world as God's handiwork must control our understanding of the relationship of the church to the world. Before ever God makes the covenant with his chosen people, he makes a covenant with all creation, assuring us that, despite his righteous judgement, it remains the object of his mercy. Instead of smugly looking out from the ark of salvation at a world sinking to its ruin, we are to remember that the ark of Noah contained within it a sample of all creatures. The rescue of Noah was in fact for the sake of the world's future. Moreover in Christ's act of re-creation, he dies, not simply for the chosen few, but for this world, to gather into one all God's scattered children. It is the world which is redeemed and not simply that small portion of it which explicitly acknowledges its redemption.

The vocation of those who belong to that small portion is to go out into the world peering for the signs of the Creator's presence and work in its midst. We may stand in a street, with the anonymous crowd swirling around us, and know that in every man, woman and child there is the spring of Holy Spirit, which, however choked by the rubbish of sin, seeks to well up to eternal life. In the hardest heart:

> the Holy Ghost
> is a poor little bird
> in a cage
> who never sings,
> and never opens his wings,
> yet never, never
> desires to be gone away.[54]

There may not be explicit response to the mystery of God, for background, upbringing and the distorting words of men may have made it well nigh impossible for that response to be made, and yet there still may be discerned movements of the soul towards the reality of eternal love in the labouring for truth, justice and beauty. Every such reaching out is in fact a reaching out towards God, a genuine, although not explicit, response to the grace of God, which is there but unrecognized. The gospels tell us that there are those who make the correct response, say the right thing, 'Lord, Lord', but who, not having made the fundamental decision for love, do not enter the kingdom. The gospels equally tell us that there are those who without recognizing Jesus yet serve him in the least of his brethren. What we have to grasp is a deeper understanding of conversion, a turning to God which is more radical and real than an assent to mere words. We assent not to notions but to the real Christ. A man can say 'yes' with his lips, but in his heart still refuse entry to that inexhaustible mystery of love which is God. A man may say 'no' with his lips, yet his heart may have opened the door to God.

No one has done more to probe the whole question of the availability of God's saving grace outside the explicit Christian enterprise than the theologian Karl Rahner. He has used the term 'anonymous Christian' to express his belief in the universality of salvation. 'The anonymous Christian . . . is the pagan after the beginning of the Christian mission who lives in the state of Christ's grace through faith, hope and love, yet who has not explicit knowledge of the fact that his life is orientated in grace-given salvation to Jesus Christ.'[55] It must be emphasized that there is no question in Rahner's mind of a salvation which bypasses the grace of Christ, no question of a 'natural' salvation. The claim is that

> even outside the Christian body there are individuals who are justified by God's grace and possess the Holy Spirit. . . The difference between this state of salvation and that of those who are Christians in an explicit sense is not such that these 'pagans' are acceptable in God's sight without any true faith (together with hope and love) as it were in virtue of a merely natural morality which they possess, whereas the Christians, and only they, achieve their justification through a faith in salvation. On the contrary the theory ascribes to these justified pagans also a real albeit unexplicated or rudimentary faith.[56]

There are those who, although sympathetic to Rahner's vision of universal salvation, are unhappy about the title 'anonymous Christian'. The Reformation tradition has been more at ease with the distinction between the church and the kingdom, and its followers perhaps happier to locate this unconscious response to God as a response which needs to be related to the kingdom. While we can say who is and who is not a member of the church, we cannot say who is and who is not near the kingdom. This way of approaching the question would, of course, meet better the other objection to the notion of 'anonymous Christians' that it impugns the seriousness and integrity of those who explicitly reject the Christian understanding. Is there not something condescending, not to say infuriating for the atheist to be told that he is 'really a Christian'? Rahner is very open in attending to such criticisms, but he sticks by his main evangelical concern, which is to affirm that salvation is in the name of Christ alone. He points out that there is often a contradiction between our living commitments and the way we understand and reflect on these commitments. It is thus possible for others to understand the implications of our commitments better than we do ourselves.

> It is obvious that a contradiction can exist between a way a person takes free possession of himself in an unthematic and unreflective manner and the way he interprets himself as an object in words and concepts, and this contradiction does not have to be noticed by the person concerned, who may indeed expressly deny it. Is it surprising that in certain circumstances the real situation and the basic self-understanding of a person may be grasped more clearly by someone else than by the person himself, who may in fact strongly resist the other's interpretation?[57]

At this point the worry arises that such a vision of universal salvation makes both gospel and church redundant and Christian mission irrelevant. Does not explicit Christianity become an optional extra? Rahner is clear that this is not the case: 'Knowledge about the anonymous Christian does not in any way dispense [us] from caring and troubling about those who do not yet know the one necessary truth in its explicit affirmation in the gospel message.'[58] 'The expressly Christian revelation' is 'the explicit statement of the revelation of grace which man always experiences implicitly in the depth of his being', but to say this is not to deny that 'the faith as it exists in the pagan is properly speaking designed to follow its inherent dynamism in such a way as to develop into that faith which is objectified and articulated through the gospel, that faith which we simply call the Christian faith. The seed has no right to seek not to grow into a plant.'[59]

The fulness of faith is to be my free and personal response to the mystery of God revealed in Jesus. In so far as my response is not conscious, has not come to know itself, it is not yet fully free. I have not yet been brought to know in whom I have believed. The description in the Acts of the Apostles (chapter 17) of St Paul in Athens does justice both to man's inarticulate groping towards the mystery of God and to the ultimate need for explicit recognition. The apostle encounters the altar to the Unknown God. He does not tear that altar down or write off the experience of the Athenian worshippers as a bleak cul-de-sac out of which they must reverse to come to the truth. He accepts what is there and builds on it. 'Whom you in ignorance worship, him we declare to you.' (Acts 17:23). The particularity of the church with its signs and words points to that unveiling of the mystery after which men have sought in many ways. The church does not believe that the saving work of God is bottled up within its confines; if Holy Spirit is its soul, he remains also the Lord, free to go where he will. He is the wind which bloweth where it listeth. But the church remains the sacrament of salvation, the sign which points to that saving work and which names the unknown one in the name which is above all other names, Jesus Christ.

It was the Second Vatican Council which provided the springboard for Karl Rahner's exciting exploration into the universality of salvation. The documents of this council give clues to a new and richer understanding of the relationship between the church and the world. The independence of the church is affirmed: 'The church, by reason of her role and competence, is not identified with any political community nor bound by ties to any political system. It is at once the sign and the safeguard of the transcendental dimension of the human person. The political community and the church are autonomous and independent of each other in their own fields.' And because the Roman Catholic church has been the recipient of the privileges and restrictions of establishment, this status is in principle clearly renounced. The church 'never places its hopes in any privileges accorded to it by civil authority; indeed it will give up the exercise of certain legitimate rights whenever it becomes clear that their use will compromise the sincerity of its witness, or whenever new circumstances call for a revised approach.'[60]

If the independence of the church is made clear, so too is its integrity as Roman Catholics understand this. The claim continues to be made that this integrity in its fulness is to be found only in communion with the see of Peter. The 'sole church of Christ . . . constituted and organised as a society in the present world subsists in the Catholic Church which is governed by the successor of Peter and by the bishops in communion with him.'[61] Yet if this view of the centre remains firm, the new understanding of it ceases to be exclusive. The council seems to see, moving outwards from this centre of unity, a number of extending circles which are related to this centre; first the 'separated brethren', then Judaism and Islam, out into the religions of the world and finally to those who have not yet faith but serve in the ways of truth, love and justice. It is made clear that although the Catholic centre is seen to be necessary for the fulness of faith and unity, it does not have a monopoly of salvation. 'Those who through no fault of their own do not know the Gospel of Christ or his church, but who nevertheless seek God with a sincere heart and, moved by grace, try in their actions to do his will as they know it through the dictates of their conscience, these too may achieve eternal salvation.'[62] In the Decree on Ecumenism, in the Declaration on the Relation of the Church to Non-Christian Religions and in the Decree on the Church's Missionary Activity, the same blend of openness to the action of God in the world and affirmation of the fulness of the Gospel is consistently met.

The Catholic Church rejects nothing in what is true and holy in these [non-christian] religions. She has a high regard for the manner of life and conduct, the precepts and doctrines which although differing in many ways from her own teaching nevertherless often reflect a ray of that truth which enlightens all men. Yet she proclaims, and is in duty bound to proclaim without fail, Christ who is the way, the truth and the life.[63]

Although in ways known to himself, God can lead those who through no fault of their own are ignorant of the Gospel to that faith without which it is impossible to please him, the church nevertheless still has the obligation and sacred duty to evangelise.[64]

The same positive approach can be seen in the council's attitude to atheism. Some, it is admitted 'have such a faulty notion of God that when they disown this product of the imagination their denial has no reference to the God of the Gospels.'[65] Indeed in the Decree on the Church this is put more positively: 'Nor shall divine providence deny the assistance necessary for salvation to those who, without any fault of theirs, have not yet arrived at an explicit knowledge of God and who, not without grace, strive to lead a good life.'[66] It will be seen that Rahner, as he seeks to open our eyes to the world as the theatre of grace, is no maverick theologian. His is a faithful exposition of Vatican 2's articulation of this remarkable revolution in the Christian consciousness.

The task of reconciling the identity and openness of the church is being taken up at the deepest theological level. Instead of dissolving the church in the world, its vocation to be sign or sacrament involves an affirmation of its identity. If it is there to speak, it must say something; if there to point, it must point somewhere. And yet all this is for the sake of a world not deprived of God but in which he is at work drawing all to himself. We have shown this openness articulated in a Roman Catholic theologian who bases himself firmly on the documents of the Second Vatican Council, but this articulation rings bells with a genuinely Anglican tradition. The Church of England may have expressed it less clearly, but its pastoral practice has shown it a treasure to be preserved. Here is an understanding of Christian mission cast in the form of pastoral care, one which respects the uniqueness and mystery of each individual person. Instead of pretending to 'bring Christ' to people, an enterprise which could surely only succeed with a dead idol, the pastor-missionary is first a contemplative who before each individual takes off his shoes, knowing that he is only holy ground. His concern is to peer into this life to perceive the action of God there. God has been at work before ever the pastor arrived on the scene. The missionary perceives that the mission is first and last the outgoing in love of God himself and that it is his vocation to be caught up in that love. Although a fellow-worker with Christ, he will not behave as if he had taken over the business. This means that there can be no taking of creed and dogma and using them as a cudgel to beat a man into submission. Not that creed and dogma are dismissed, leaving us to make up our own religion: the sign has to point firmly to the fulness of God's revelation in Christ, which can never be cut down to what Jones can here and now take. But it is an abuse of the unsearchable riches of Christ to ram them all at once down our throats. The ways of God are patient ways as he leads us into all truth. The pastor-missionary knows that he must go at God's pace. Here and now there are to be discerned the divine openings, the small shafts of truth which have come alive for this unique person. 'Don't worry about all the things you cannot believe. Start with what God has shown you and then move forward and never stop.' That is how smoking flax is fanned into a full flame.

Such is the openness and gentleness of the Anglican pastoral tradition which, I believe, the Bishop of Durham and I have in common. With him, I see this inheritance threatened by insensitive forms of evangelism and a fearful dogmatism. But what will really strengthen that which we both labour to preserve? Assuredly not the establishment, with its counterfeit openness suggesting that, despite everything, England remains deep-down Christian, and C of E at that; not that national Christianity which offers the gifts of grace without calling for hard decision and commitment. I see no sign in such genial establish-mentarianism of the ability to take seriously the claims of both holiness and catholicity or of the struggle to reconcile them. Indeed, to lean upon the broken reed of the state connection with its redundant and therefore distorting symbols prevents us from engaging in the real task of digging to that rock of the gospel, the holy catholicity of Christ himself.

3 Establishment — Good for the Nation?

A church could have all the freedom it wanted but be so tied up in the search for its own purity and integrity that it forgot the gospel warning: 'Whoever seeks to gain his life will lose it.' The church lives safely only by giving itself away, by being stamped with the mark of the Servant who washes the feet of the world. So that, even if no great benefits accrue to the church through its ties with the state, attention must be paid to the claim that it is good for the nation. Establishment might have to be accepted if it were of service to the world.

It is argued that the bonds which tie the church to the state bear witness to the unity of the nation under God. Establishment does not allow us to claim the church for God while letting politics go to the devil. Matters secular are held under the ultimate rule of God by a number of powerful symbols. The sovereign, who is both head of state and Supreme Governor of the Church of England, is crowned by the Archbishop of Canterbury. Some of the bishops of the established church sit in the high court of Parliament. The business of political debate is preceded in both Houses by acts of prayer led by the clergy of the national church. National occasions are celebrated in the great shrines of the established church. These symbols, it is argued, show that the nation officially acknowledges Christian beliefs and values. So the Bishop of Durham believes that disestablishment would be bad for the nation 'because now of all times, we need in our nation, some continuing acknowledgements of religious belief and sanctions to give us direction.'

It is easier to grasp the theory than to see that it works in practice. Members of the House of Commons do not show a notable enthusiasm for their daily acts of devotion and it is difficult, in attending a debate, to detect any consciousness of legislating in the presence and under the judgement of God. What difference to the ethos, let alone to the outcome, of parliamentary debate would it make if these daily devotions were abolished? At this point supporters of establishment are apt to point to somewhat elusive streams of healing which are alleged to pass into the life of the nation through the ties between church and state. A mysterious 'X' is added to the quality of the national life, of which countries labouring under the disability of disestablishment are deprived. It is all very difficult to grasp. Are the moral standards of the English manifestly better than those of the Welsh? Studies of religious practice, belief and morality in Europe do not reveal particularly high ratings in those countries which have established churches. Indeed, while Sweden and England have become something of a byword for secularism, it would not take a very sophisticated study to reveal that the Poles were more believing than the English. The theory that society benefits from an established church looks promising but, by any test of effectiveness one may devise, it is difficult to discover evidence that it works. It seems a rather desperate move on the part of the establishmentarian to fall back on the assertion that matters would be even worse were the church disestablished.

Of course symbols can be very important, but they have to be living symbols which point to some reality. Thus the state opening of Parliament continues to work because its symbols continue to say something which is still true and important about the constitution. If the symbols of establishment were earthed in some reality, we could say the same about them, but the fact is that they increasingly have the appearance of religious icing on top of a fairly secular cake. And if that be the case, then we are left, not simply with harmless and amusing ornaments but mischievous purveyors of nostalgia which inhibit us from coming to terms with reality. It is sometimes said that the English have a taste for ceremonial of doubtful meaning — it brings colour to an otherwise drab century. Perhaps bishops dressed up in their convocation robes sitting in the House of Lords could be seen as that. In fact one of the most delightful though meaningless ceremonies of the establishment is that rarely witnessed event, the 'confirmation' of a bishop's election. At this, after the saying of the litany, lawyers set to to prove that the elected candidate, who has not in fact been elected in any intelligible sense of that word, is the man he is alleged to be. Movements are being made to abolish it but in truth it has all the good clean fun of the Mad Hatter's Tea Party. Many such oddities can be justified for the innocent amusement they bring; reformers must beware of being dour and humourless about them but must equally recognize that there comes a point when redundant symbols prevent us from seeing what is in fact the case. To put it simply, if the symbols of establishment suggest that the nation deep down holds Christian beliefs, affirms Christian values and offers Christian worship when, for the most part, it does none of these things, then the symbols frankly encourage delusion, and delusion is always a barrier to spiritual advance. Repentance and new life depend on facing how in fact we stand before God. Of course we may gratefully acknowledge that streams of healing do flow into the life of nations from the churches, but they do not flow simply from established churches. In this country as great a contribution comes from the Free Churches and the Roman Catholic Church as from the Church of England. The Christian creativity of the churches in Poland, South Africa and Latin America springs notably from those without official status or acknowledgement.

The Bishop of Durham's words, 'now at all times', indicate that he sees in the present stresses of our society a particular need for this 'continuing acknowledgement of religious beliefs and sanctions'. If I understand him aright, he is drawing attention to the fragility of our liberal democratic society. The old 'consensus politics' are increasingly rejected by both right and left. The right seeks to roll back the frontiers of the state and revive that more individualistic and enterprising spirit of nineteenth-century laissez-faire liberalism, while the left sees the good society emerging only as a result of laying bare the conflict which lies hidden beneath consensus and facing the radical disturbance which is necessary. A new abrasive and divisive quality has crept into English politics, which flourishes in those cracks in society which recession and unemployment have opened up. While those on the far right and left see this as a necessary moment of truth, others fear that the strain may prove too great for our tolerant liberal democracy. The threat of a totalitarian state, whether of national emergency or of workers' revolution, becomes something more than a nasty nightmare. There are those who see the need to locate and strengthen bonds of national unity. Clearly the monarchy is one such bond, but the Church of England could be another. Here is an institution with branches throughout the country, to which many still turn in times of joy and grief, which can act as a social bond, a bulwark against anarchy and disorder. It is not necessary to share its beliefs to be convinced that the Church of England could play such a valuable role.

The reality of this view has to be tested. While there remain many areas in the gentle south, in market towns and villages where the local church, if all too rarely visited, is still somewhere to come home to celebrate marriage and birth and to mourn one's dead, there are other parts of the country, the down-town areas of industrial cities and the bleak council housing estates, where this sense of belonging no longer exists. It is a proven and notorious fact that it is in precisely these areas of greatest social stress and need that the national church is at its weakest. The truth is that, instead of the church bonding together a fragmented society, it is itself a reflection of that fragmentation. How can a church which so often mirrors the division between Surrey and Sunderland, market town and industrial city, itself be the agent of healing? As we face this uncomfortable truth, the symbols of establishment can mesmerize and distract us. There is enthusiasm for a royal wedding; not only are there jolly street parties but there is the Archbishop of Canterbury preaching to the nation. Deep down all things are well, all manner of things are well! Yet when the party is over, the real divisions are still there. The deep division between those parts of the country which are easy on the eye, in which men go to work and their families enjoy reasonable educational and health services, and those areas of grey graffiti-adorned buildings, with 60 per cent of youth unemployed and social services which can no longer cope — that division still remains. Class division is not a figment of the imagination; it is real, hideous, irrational and above all dehumanizing, for it deprives us of the gifts and friendships of other people. Such wounds cannot be lightly healed with a few genial symbols. Our society is fragmented and the fragmentation threatens liberal democracy; the bitter truth has to be faced and healing sought at a level deeper than that reached by the romantic image of establishment.

Without being over-dramatic, we take the dangers of our society seriously but believe that they constitute a further reason for breaking the formal ties between church and state. If overnight this country were engulfed by a totalitarian regime, every Christian church would be threatened, for there is no church so free and independent as to be immune from the danger of being used by a determined government. Enforced ecumenism might well serve the interests of the state, and well-intentioned churchmen, frustrated by the inability of the churches to heal themselves, might be beguiled by statesmen succeeding where synods have failed. Yet a church with existing state ties, whose chief officers can still be chosen by the prime minister and whose liturgical performance can be the subject of Parliamentary censure, is clearly more at risk than any other. It is sobering to listen to a German Christian recalling the almost imperceptible way in which that national church found itself taken over and used by the Nazis. Who, hearing that tale, can doubt that the church which best served the nation in that crisis was the sturdy independent Confessing Church, which perceived its main service as the preservation of the integrity of the gospel? Although in the past such tales have been met with a stubborn belief in the indestructibility of English institutions, the Bishop of Durham shows no such complacency. Indeed it takes no heated imagination to contemplate a scenario in which a government of national security found itself appealing to 'traditional values', attacking permissiveness and calling for a more bracing discipline. With such a bait dangled before them, who could be sure that there would be no church leaders, no rank-and-file Christians, who would not fall for it and thus find themselves acquiescing in the suppression of all manner of civil liberties? If such a threat be not unreal, there is reason while there is still time to distance ourselves further from the organ of government.

So far we have considered alleged social benefits of establishment, which, by their very vagueness, elude careful scrutiny. It is with some relief that we now come down to earth to consider one particular aspect of the church—state relationship. Along with the Archbishops of Canterbury and York, twenty-four senior bishops sit by right in the House of Lords. Here, at least, is a point where establishment can be evaluated and might prove to be of service to the nation.

There are many ways in which the bishops have used this privilege creatively. They behave with ecumenical sensitivity, knowing that their position can be justified only if they try to become spokesmen for all the churches. In recent years their contributions to important debates have sprung from careful consultation with other Christians. Moreover, there has been a widening of their social concern, so that they have spoken, not only on matters of personal morality, but on such topics as housing, unemployment and the social services. In this way they have risked their political neutrality. Both ecumenical sensitivity and wide social concern came together in their admirable opposition to the Nationality Bill. Some bishops took their opposition to the point of voting against the government. I have a personal memory of the way a bishop can take the opportunities which membership of the House of Lords affords. When I was vicar of a colliery parish back in the 1960s, the local miners' lodge, in protest against the pit closures which were taking place under the then Labour government, withdrew the political levy. It was a matter of some excitement and debate in the parish, with events culminating on the day of the Durham Miners' Gala, when members of the colliery band were instructed to withdraw their instruments from their lips as they passed the prime minister standing on the balcony of the County Hotel. Although the lodge members were dismissed by the Labour Party establishment as wild hotheads, Ian Ramsey, then Bishop of Durham, came to listen to their sharply expressed views and was later, in the House of Lords able to articulate them. The impact in the colliery was considerable. There was a strong feeling that their bishop had spoken for them in a way no politician had done. In this and in many other ways, the bishops have shown themselves able to use the opportunities which the House of Lords affords. Furthermore, despite the fact that the debate on the Prayer Book Protection Bill revealed some suspicion, which bordered at times on hostility towards the bishops, many peers con-continue to testify to the value they see in having the bishops in the Lords. It is not always quite clear what is most appreciated, but one suspects that it is often that the chief pastors of the church take the opportunity to minister in a personal way to those who bear the responsibility and isolation of power. This pastoral care may be more valued than anything the bishops may say in the chamber.

Archbishop Michael Ramsey regretted that 'the Chadwick Report did not probe into the question of the value and importance of the bishops' contemporary role in the House of Lords.' He wished 'that the Commission had explored how far membership of the House of Lords is the most suitable and effective forum for the bishops' influence in moral and social questions today.'[67] If one is to make such a tentative exploration, it is necessary to distinguish between two possible ways of exercising Christian influence. There is first what we may, rather loosely, call the 'prophetic role' of bearing witness to the demands and values of the kingdom of God and perceiving how the standards of society measure up to these values. This proclamation of the judging and redeeming Word of God is clearly the primary task of bishops as ministers of that Word. It needs to be emphasized that, in the Christian view of things, this is more than 'mere idealism', for the rule of God to which we point is what is believed to be most really real, that which beneath the layers of sin, is in fact the case. The prophet thus calls not for a flight from reality but adjustment to it. Now it is obvious that, in the House of Lords, bishops have the opportunity to exercise such a ministry. Yet the practical question must be asked: 'To whom are they trying to speak, whom are they seeking to influence? Simply their fellow peers or are they reaching out to a wider audience?' In a liberal democracy such as ours, in which leaders cannot edge too far beyond public opinion, the Christian word to be effective has to capture the imagination, mind and conscience of the nation at large. So there arises a very simple question about whether the hours spent in the Lords are really worth it for this purpose. Is the Upper House a good platform for those who wish to address the nation? The fact has to be faced that the fullest press report will reduce the Bishop of Barchester's pearls of wisdom to a few lines. If the bishop wants to 'speak out' he might be better employed on the Jimmy Young show. It is interesting to note with Archbishop Ramsey that 'William Temple, who is often upheld as a kind of exemplar of the Church's prophetic witness, took very little part in the Lords throughout the years of his member-ship.'[67]

If the prophetic is one Christian role, the political is another. Here it is that we turn from pointing the direction in which society ought to move to the labour of working out what faltering step, here and now, we can take in that direction. In taking up this task, we wrestle with the realities of power and seek to make effective our vision of the good society. Although there are Christians who seem content to hug their vision to themselves in the purity of a wilderness uncontaminated by politics, this indicates not faithfulness but a dilution of the rule of God into a mere ideal, a loss of confidence in the fact that the ways of God are the ways to a true and solid justice. Although the Upper House has only a limited power, it has shown, by its ability to modify government policy, that it is more than a 'talking shop'. But the fact of the matter is that political muscle lies more often in the committee rooms than on the floor of the House, so that the question is: if the bishops are to engage in serious political action, how feasible is it for them to be involved in such time-consuming service? Looking at our bishops' already over-packed diaries, we may conclude that the impossible is being demanded and that here we have stumbled upon a role confusion. While some Christians must respond to the political vocation, bishops may not be the right people to do it.

While prophetic and political roles are both legitimate Christian ministries, there is not much to be said for falling between the two stools and occupying a sort of middle-ground in which we neither firmly announce the demands of the kingdom nor full-bloodedly engage in political action. It is the middle region in which Christians so often gather to engage in endless discussion on politics when they might be dispersed as members of the political parties of their choice. The nation cannot be served by playing at politics. It may be said that bishops in the House of Lords, dressed up in their convocation robes, advertise to the nation the presence of the church in secular affairs. But it is this lust for advertisement, this desire to be 'seen' to be involved, which has to be questioned. When it comes to politics, it is power and not the appearance of power which matters.

The church's witness in the world is defined by him whose lordship was cast in the form of a servant. His word to the leaders of the Christian community is clear: their leadership is to be different from secular leadership. 'The kings of the Gentiles exercise lordship over them and those in authority over them are called benefactors. But not so with you; rather let the greatest among you become as the youngest and the leader as one who serves.' (Luke 22:25, 26) The form this service has taken in response to that word has varied in particular circumstances. So there have been periods of history which can be described as 'ages of faith', not of course in the sense that all members of society were personally convinced Christians, but that society consciously tried to set before itself the values and standards of Christ. Performance always fell far short of aspiration, but here was a framework which could be called explicitly Christian. It is that framework which has now disintegrated. Instead of common faith and values we have competing faiths and values. Instead of having one 'corner shop' or general stores with its limited range of goods, the consumer now feels free to shop around in a supermarket of faiths and values.

No longer can the half-hearted rely on being held by the old framework or carried by the tides of custom and convention into a formal adherence to Christianity. All of us feel a real freedom and obligation to make up our own minds and decide for ourselves. It is important that the situation in which we find ourselves be treated as neither an unmitigated evil nor utopia. The secular city is neither the realm of Satan nor the kingdom of God. In so far as the weaker brethren are carried further from the influence of faith, it is an ill, but in so far as we are given a new chance to make a free decision for Christ, it is good. Like all human situations it is ambiguous, but what is not ambiguous is God's call to be present at this time. On this Karl Rahner insists:

> The fact that the church is becoming a diaspora everywhere, that she is a church surrounded by non-Christians, and hence living in a culture, in a state, amidst political movements, economic activity, science and art which are conducted not simply and solely by Christians — all this is a 'must' in the history of salvation.[68]

We have not only to acknowledge this diaspora situation as unfortunately permitted by God, but can recognise it as willed by God as a 'must' (not as an 'ought').[69]

It is this attention, without despair or euphoria, to the present moment which is the burden of so much Christian spiritual writing: 'The present moment is always the ambassador who declares the order of God. . . The "one thing necessary" is always to be found by the soul in the present moment.'[70] The message of the eighteenth-century French spiritual writer, de Caussade, that we have to be where God sets us down, has to be taken as seriously in our politics as in our prayer. To be in the world as Jesus would have us be is neither to indulge in nostalgia for a golden past, nor to dream of an utopian future, the here and now, the situation as it is, is our post.

This grasp of the present moment makes us ask more urgently, 'What is the appropriate form of Christian involvement in the world?' The bishops in the House of Lords are symbolic figures but the trouble is that the symbols are saying the wrong things. They speak of a clerical and labelled Christian presence in the affairs of the nation at a time when the situation calls for a presence which is lay and anonymous. While bishops are in the House of Lords because they are bishops, in a pluralist society influence is exercised not by who you are but by your degree of competence and understanding of the situation. The fact that some bishops are, amidst all their other duties, almost miraculously competent is a bonus, but beside the point. The spotlight falls in the wrong place. The symbol encourages the still lingering belief that, for the church to be present, a clergyman has to be wheeled in. We politely acknowledge the royal priesthood of the laity but, continuing to act on clericalist assumptions, remain blind to the immense potential of the church in the world. Instead of for ever going on about 'sending Christians out into the world', praying those terrible 'heave ho and out we go' prayers which are such a lamentable feature of our modern liturgies, the need is to recognize that Christians are willy-nilly in the world and that the real task is to convince them that they, and not a gaggle of priests, are there the agents and representatives of Christ. The church is present where they are present. What we have lost in terms of advertisement, we have gained in terms of effectiveness, for the church present in its laity is more deeply immersed in particular situations and thus less likely to escape into woolly generalizations. The anonymity of this presence is gain, not loss, a presence more faithful to the gospel images of the yeast hidden in the dough or the unseen salt. Here is Kierkegaard's 'knight of faith', the ordinary man who merges with the crowd, who looks like an inspector of taxes, who makes 'the movement of infinity . . . with such precision and assurance that he possesses himself of the finite without anyone suspecting anything else'.[71] Here is the disciple whose life is hid with Christ in God, whose faith is forged in the secret place. If the removal of bishops from the House of Lords were to be read as the church opting out of the life of the nation, that would only show what a wrong and muddled idea of the church's involvement we have projected through such symbols.

In probing the role of bishops in the House of Lords we see the danger of the tasks of prophecy and politics being distorted by the church—state link and Christians slipping into a middle region which is neither seriously prophetic nor political. That this is not the only situation in which the edge is taken off prophecy and realism drained from politics can be illustrated in some of the issues which confront us.

The church continues to worry at the problem of marriage and divorce. Here it is called to the prophetic task of stating that the reality of marriage is in lifelong commitment and to the pastoral task of caring for broken personal relationships. It is easy to sneer at the church's present practice. Clergymen, having steeled themselves to refuse a second marriage in church, then go on to allow or even encourage a service of blessing after a civil marriage. It looks dangerously like nonsense but there is in fact an instinctive wisdom in this muddled pastoral approach. The affirmation that marriage is a lifelong commitment would be seriously weakened if the same service and the same vows were to be used in the case of such marriages. In marriage a man and woman are to love as Christ loved his spouse the church, to love each other in the way Christ has loved us. That way of the love of God is a commitment to us without reservation or drawing back. The high vocation of embodying this faithful love of God requires lifelong commitment. To modify or to weaken this affirmation would be to sell the world short of what God has to offer. There is, of course, in this understanding of marriage a healthy realism about the power of the sexual instinct for creativity or for destruction. It needs to be held within strong and secure bonds. That should need no arguing as, in our society, we contemplate the tragic consequences of love left to the none too tender mercies of fluctuating passion. Not harshness but mercy keeps the church faithful in making this affirmation.

But pastors know that marriages break down. Sometimes it is for trivial reasons, sometimes because of deep personality disorders, sometimes through sheer selfishness or a lazy unwillingness to work at problems, but always what happens is, even for the apparently hard-boiled, more tragic and wounding than they ever imagined. God does not wash his hands of these situations; he continues to love us in our sin and failure, and where God is the church must be, encouraging couples who have entered into a second union, often after great care and thought, to believe in the presence of God in their lives, his offer of forgiveness and the possibility of genuine new life. Care has to be taken that the church's affirmation of God's mercy is made with great truthfulness. It is possible that a church wedding or even a service of blessing can be used to cover a past which has to be faced. Forgiveness does not mean that the past no longer exists. Hope for the future depends on being reconciled to it. Falteringly the Church of England tries to do justice to both God's creative intention for marriage and his continued presence in the lives of those whose marriages have broken down and who seek a new relationship. A second marriage in church, involving a repetition of vows taken once before, is refused, but then the divorced and remarried are welcomed to our altars and blessings given to civil marriages. It is a workable response to a complex problem, but one which could be improved were the privileges and disabilities of the established church in the matter of marriage to be removed.

Although the present discipline of the church, as I have stated it, has been reaffirmed by the General Synod on several occasions, it has never been set out in canon law. In law a priest is quite free to solemnize the marriage of a divorced person. The reason why this discipline has never been enshrined in the church's official law is that canon law is the law of the land and, because the state accepts divorce, any such law would involve a contradiction. Thus while Canon B 30 can state 'The Church of England affirms, according to our Lord's teaching, that marriage is in its nature a union permanent and life-long', the consequences of this affirmation cannot be followed up in Canon B 31 on impediments to marriage. The status of canon law has made it impossible for the church to articulate its own discipline. Does this much matter? I think that it does, in so far as it becomes clearer that the working out of a better marriage discipline, which is both firm and compassionate, requires the disentanglement of the church's understanding of marriage from that of the state. Although the state continues to encourage the view that marriage is a lifelong commitment, ever easier divorce laws have in practice undermined it. It now needs to be recognized that church and state have parted company in their respective understandings of marriage. Pastors who have talked to young couples before marriage know that this is how it is perceived. Why be married in church? Because, we are told, a marriage in a registry office does not commit you in the same way as one in a church. This fact can and should be faced in a way which is sympathetic to the state's dilemma. It does not want to weaken the institution of marriage, but it has, in some measure, to reflect the widely differing views on sex and marriage which exist in a pluralist society in which the Christian view is not the only one. But, of course, by the same token the church must have the freedom to establish its own standards. This would involve the end of the particular privileges and duties which the Church of England at present enjoys. The parish priest would no longer have the dubious privilege of acting the part of the registrar nor the obligation to marry any two persons one of whom is resident in the parish. The privilege is one which few parish priests would abandon with cries of agony, while the obligation is a known recipe for pastoral irresponsibility. What priest, faced with a couple of starry-eyed teenagers, has not seen that pastoral responsibility requires the freedom to say 'no' as well as 'yes'? As our Free Church and Roman Catholic brethren have shown, there is no need for this freedom to be used in a rigorist way, but it does make possible the offer of a distinctively Christian understanding of marriage to those who wish freely to accept it. Were this divergence between church and state honestly acknowledged, the context in which the church would have to rethink its own discipline would be dramatically changed and a new flexibility given. At the moment, the tension between the prophetic vocation to affirm and the pastoral vocation to accept, which is difficult enough in any case, is complicated by the pretence that church and nation share the same view of marriage. Such disentanglement would in no way imply that the church was less concerned for the quality of marriage in society. The church would be able more clearly to render the nation its primary service by bearing witness to the reality of marriage as intended by God, that high vocation to embody the committed love of God himself. The church would also, fully accepting the 'must' of witnessing in a pluralist society, instead of nagging about divorce laws, support whatever institutions and laws strengthened marriage. It could be both clear in the articulation of its faith and concerned in caring for all human relationships as they are.

Since the beginning of 1982 there has been a more overt tension between church and state over the matter of nuclear disarmament. The report of a working party of the Board for Social Responsibility of the General Synod caused a remarkable reaction. It is not every day that such reports become the subject of leaders in newspapers, parliamentary questions and governmental condemnation. Usually they can be dismissed as the harmless ravings of idealists who are, in fact, quite nice to have around as long as they stick to the wilderness. The trouble with *The Church and the Bomb* was that it did not rest content with principles but dared to explore how these principles might be translated into practice. It was the dangerous but necessary movement from prophecy to politics.

The prophetic word about modern warfare needs to be sharp and uncompromising. As the report showed this is not necessarily to opt for the minority witness of pacifism but to apply in present-day circumstances the traditional concept of a just war, which held that there are limits to what human beings can do to each other even in the horrors of war. It was, of course, only by drawing on such an insight that the Nuremberg trials of the German war criminals could be justified. If in war there are 'no holds barred', there could be no 'war criminals'. It is the case that in maintaining this view we have given a sadly Canute-like appearance, withdrawing with high-minded protests every time the technology of war has developed and new horrors have been fashioned. Yet faithfulness to this tradition will have us go on insisting that, however difficult, a line must be drawn. The fact that we have already passed over the threshold of what is morally acceptable, not only in the bombing of Hiroshima and Nagasaki, but also in the obliteration bombing of the German cities, is no argument for Canute to move his throne a few more paces back to allow the unacceptable to become acceptable. Seeing what we have done, we know that we have already gone too far. The line has been passed and we know that the use of nuclear weapons would push us even further beyond that line. Their use would be immoral and the threat to use them therefore as immoral as the threat to do anything immoral. A clear and simple 'no' to this is required; as clear and simple as it should be to any contemplated action which is intrinsically evil — as clear as the 'no' to rape, or to the kidnapping of innocent people by some terrorist gang in the pursuit of what it believes to be a good end. One recalls that

churchmen were invited to condemn in no uncertain terms
the violent mobs of Toxteth in 1982. Nothing, we were
told, could justify such behaviour. It is precisely that sort of
'no' which great movements like the Campaign for Nuclear
Disarmament have been articulating. Nuclear warfare, like
kidnapping and assassination, can be justified by nothing.
It is very important that this simple 'no' to moral iniquity
should not be blunted. Civilized society depends on this,
the ability of ordinary people to see the wood for the trees
and to know sin when they see it. When a Foreign Office
internal document is quoted as saying that 'giving a moral
lead may be good for the conscience but it is not a valid
proposition in the real world', IRA terrorists might be
heard muttering 'Amen'. Bishop Butler rightly interpreted
the Foreign Office as meaning 'a "good" end justifies
whatever may seem to contribute to it', and pertinently
asked 'Is a nation which thus turns its back on the
categorical imperatives of morality worth preserving?'[72] We
dare not dismiss such moral simplicity as a mere spasm of
emotion, nor lose its straightforward point in a maze of
sophistication. Of course the concept of the 'non-combatant'
can be eroded by the observation, true in itself, that not all
non-combatants are really such. If it is permissible to kill
soldiers why not munition workers? Yet, as the pitiful sight
of dead Lebanese women and children showed, we all
recognized non-combatants when we saw them. As the
report puts it: 'The fact that there are doubtful cases must
not be allowed to paralyse judgement. Most cases are not
doubtful.'[73] Indeed it is the paralyzing of the moral
judgement of ordinary people by a web of political
complexity that we must most fear. We are not to be bullied
by sneers at our instinctive 'no' into handing over responsibility for moral judgement to a small group of experts who
know all the intricacies of nuclear strategy and all the
political options. 'The great man, the true prophet,' wrote
John Robinson, 'is the man who can see the moral issue as
simple as it is — as simple as Jesus always saw it — and the
political issue as complex as it is.'[74] If we do not always
know what to do next, we know more often than is

comfortable what we must not do, and we know it with awful simplicity and force.

Yet the second part of that quotation from John Robinson is as important as the first. If the moral issue is simple the political issue is complex. We deceive ourselves if we imagine that by registering our moral protest we have solved the political problem. 'Ban the Bomb' is not politics; it is a moral stance which awaits political implementation. There is no doubt that we have to move from protest to politics, from pointing the way to discovering what steps we can, here and now, take along that way. It is in fact irresponsible for the protester to refuse to engage in such questions. Having willed the end, he must join in the search for means. It is no good pretending that the independent deterrent or American bases will disappear overnight with a wave of the magic wand. In fact the strength of the report *The Church and the Bomb* was that it made the clear moral stand and then dared to advance into the area of political action. This is risky business, for when it comes to political programmes the church has no divine authority or wisdom, and the working party's suggestions may prove mistaken. Yet, in so chancing its arm, the working party did what the church's critics say it often fails to do: wrestled with the question of the next practical step. It is assuredly this movement from prophecy to politics, this care for effective action, which alarmed government circles and brought such a vigorous response. No clearer evidence could have been given that the report was on target. Those who reject the report's unilateralist position need now urgently to show that the existing policies are capable of delivering the goods and leading to the beginning of the dismantling of the nuclear armoury. The ball is in the court of the multi-lateralists, the credibility of whose policies now depends on some move in what we all agree to be the right direction. The case for the deterrent cannot go on resting on the achievement of uneasy peace between the great power blocs; it has to show that the vicious spiral of the nuclear arms race can be stopped.

The irritation which some politicians have shown with

the church over *The Church and the Bomb* may be but a symptom of an increasingly uneasy relationship. The truth is that many Christians find themselves out of sympathy with the direction in which our society is, at present, being pointed. This is, in all honesty, not a conflict which the church has generated. Since the Second World War some measure of agreement has existed in Great Britain on the sort of society we want. We were committed to the welfare state and thus to the belief that society should and could move forward from the rewarding of the successful to a care for the unsuccessful and victims of society. Health services and education, we agreed, should be available for all, regardless of wealth or merit. Of course it was all very inadequate, but Christians saw in this some embodiment of their conviction that individual people matter supremely. Society could begin to be shaped to express the insight that individuals are valuable, not because they are clever, able, successful, or even good, but because as human beings they are made in the image and likeness of God whose children they are. In this sense the common vision was egalitarian. We shared the view of the American humanist Walter Lippmann:

> There you are sir, and there is your neighbour. You are better born than he, you are richer, or you are stronger, you are handsomer, nay, you are better, wiser, kinder, more likeable; you have given more to your fellowman and taken less than he. By any and every test of intelligence, of virtue, of usefulness, you are demonstrably a better man than he, and yet — absurd as it sounds — these differences do not matter, for the best part of him is untouchable and incomparable and unique and universal. Either you feel this or you do not; when you do not feel it the superiorities that the world acknowledges seem like mountainous waves at sea; when you do feel it they are slight and impermanent ripples upon a vast ocean.[75]

It is true that the political right was suspicious of the word 'equality', fearing that it suggested a squashing out of individual variety, and thus preferred to emphasize the 'freedom' of the individual to become a unique fulfilled person. However the debate was largely a matter of words, and few doubted that society should treat its citizens as being of equal value and each given the opportunity to achieve his or her unique fulfilment. We were working at reconciling the claims of equality and freedom and, in doing so, forged bonds of fraternity. It was this, not the symbols of monarchy or established church, which created a real measure of national unity. The remarkable thing was the way in which this common vision cut across the lines of party political division. There was plenty of debate about means to achieve this end, but little serious doubting of the end itself.

Over the past few years we have seen an attempt to dismantle this common vision. It has been seen by right and left as a phoney unity, a papering over of real cracks. The far left never liked the smell of consensus politics, but it has taken a government of the right to rob it of its respectability. Our faces have been turned back to the nineteenth-century virtues of hard work, initiative, struggle and success. No doubt some such bracing qualities were needed, but the awful irony is that the summons to such endeavour goes out to a growing number of unemployed, who are unable to respond. The new direction may call forth all sorts of desirable qualities, but there is a heavy price to pay and the payment of that price falls upon those least able to bear it. It is those who live in areas which have already to bear the strain and stress of poverty, inadequate housing, street violence and racism who are in receipt of the heaviest doses of this medicine. Supporters of the new way say that these are but the birth pangs of economic and social regeneration. Belts must be tightened and harsh discipline endured for the sake of a brighter future.

In the political climate of 1983, the debate swings from means to ends, from how best to achieve a common goal to what the goal should be. R.H. Tawney commented:

It is a commonplace that the characteristic virtue of Englishmen is their power of sustained practical activity and their characteristic vice a reluctance to test the quality of that activity by reference to principles. They are incurious as to theory, take fundamentals for granted and are more interested in the state of the roads than in their place on the map.

Tawney granted that this 'combination of intellectual tameness with practical energy 'was at most times a serviceable combination' but, he went on,

if the medicine of the constitution might not be made its daily food, neither can its daily food be made medicine. There are times which are not ordinary and in such times it is not enough to follow the road. It is necessary to know where it leads and, if it leads nowhere, to find another.[76]

We clearly find ourselves at such a time involved willy-nilly in a debate about the direction of our society.

There are still some who think that the church should keep above such a debate. Priests are called to stick to their proper business of offering divine worship and preaching the gospel. Indeed in this lies our primary service to the nation but our worship cannot be insulated from the world nor do we preach into a vacuum. In our worship we reach out towards the Holy God but, as we do so we glimpse the materials of this world, bread and wine, transformed into the life of Christ; praying 'Thy kingdom come,' there is stirred within us the uncomfortable longing that the kingdoms of this world should become the kingdom of this same Christ. The word that we preach, if it be the Word of the true and living God, is no mere word 'but that which going forth returneth not empty but accomplishes that which God purposes' (Isaiah 55:10,11). It is to be an echo of the Word which made those who heard Jesus exclaim, 'What is this? A new teaching! With authority he commands unclean spirits and they obey him.' (Mark 1:22)

Just as our worship cannot be sealed up in a cultic box neither can our gospel be reduced to mere beautiful thoughts. It is precisely when we stick to our worship and our gospel that we shall find ourselves thrust into the debate about society. The fuss about the Falkland Islands service showed this. There the issue was, not whether the service reflected the mood of the nation, but whether it was a faithful vehicle of the Word of God. Politicians who say that the church is not in business to be trendy are correct; we are to be swept along neither by trends to the left nor to the right — our duty is simply to hear the Word of God and keep it. The trouble is that that Word has and always has had political implications for it is a Word not simply to inspire but to make all things new, societies as well as individuals. The critics of Christian involvement in politics do not really understand what sort of thing the gospel is. They operate with a practical dualism, handing the soul over to the church while believing that the devil reigns over the body politic; the demands of Christ are simply a set of fine ideals to which the individual should aspire, but which he can attain only in heaven. They do not see that what Christ declares is the revelation of ultimate reality. 'Competition,' wrote F.D. Maurice, 'is set forth as the law of the universe. That is a lie.'[77] Not, you note, a mistaken ideal, but a lie, a denial of the way things really are. The law of fallen man is 'every man for himself', but we are called to dig beneath this fallenness to the more fundamental reality of our creation and redemption in him in whose image we are made and through whom that image is restored. 'Society is not to be made anew by arrangements of ours, but is to be regenerated by finding the law and ground of its order and harmony, the only secret of its existence, in God.'[78] That foundation of all human life is God the Holy Trinity, 'the eternal charity', God in the perfect co-operation of Father, Son and Holy Spirit who in equality yet retain the integrity of their unique 'persons'. This what Christians believe to be the ultimate fact of the matter. Those who labour for human unity, knowing that unless we learn to live together we shall die together, but tempted to believe that co-operation is just a fine ideal destined to be crucified by the forces of division in the world, can find hope in the gospel just because it witnesses to the fact that reality is on the side of justice and peace.

In the last resort politicians will not be much troubled if the church sticks to the business of 'speaking out'. A niche for idealists can always be found as long as they keep safely on the mantelpiece reserved for such ornaments. The sparks begin to fly when Christians insist on being effective and so get into the meat of politics. A concern for how we achieve what we want to achieve is as necessary as a clear vision of the goal. The common vision of the compassionate society has been endangered because its supporters cared for ends and neglected means. The Conservative Party swept to power less because the nation had lost faith in a common vision than because it had lost faith in the left's ability to fund it.

The political right must take credit for having got the message home that the welfare state is expensive, indeed that it consumes ever more and more resources, so that, at a time of world recession, we have to labour ever harder to produce the resources. On the left there was a fastidiousness about wealth creation, an eagerness to see that eggs were fairly distributed, combined with a tendency to kick the goose which laid what golden eggs were available. Even now, the attempts of the Conservative government to wrestle with the well-nigh overwhelming problem of wealth creation in the recession, have been met by the left's somewhat aristocratic disdain for trade; donnish socialists cannot disguise their dislike for shopkeepers. If the compassionate society is to be saved and regenerated we shall need practical visionaries with as much care for egg production as distribution. It is here that the very purity of our vision can hinder its implementation. Those who are committed to the welfare state will have to combine a resoluteness about the goal with less dogmatism and more flexibility about means. Can we really afford to look down our noses at the contribution to health and education which might come from private resources? Just as the left had to come to terms with prescription charges, so it may have to do the same over a wider range of matters. The Conservatives have made their point: this sort of society costs money and pennies will not drop from heaven. It is in this practical political task of finding how to edge a few paces forward towards our goal that Christians must be involved.

This, of course, does not mean a Christian political party or a self-conscious Christian pressure group; the service will be exercised by the church in dispersion, by individual Christians scattered throughout the political parties of the land. If they seem to gravitate towards the 'wet' middle, this will be because their common vision of a society made for people finds itself up against a Marxism to the left which would make people the servants of the state and a monetarism to the right which would fit people into the "demands" of the economy. From all parties they will make common cause in the belief that both state and economy are made for man.

To pursue a prophetic and a political vocation is not easy, yet if the church struggles with this it can do so in the assurance that it is working at one of the main problems of our society. Amongst all our divisions, the one which could prove most dangerous is that between idealists and realists. Divided from one another, idealists may be left in the wilderness hugging their vision, while politicians will plod on in a hand-to-mouth way, without any sense of direction. The church has had long experience of living with the problem, caught as it is between the total demands of the kingdom embodied in the life and teaching of Jesus and the need to attend to the requirements of the present moment. The main stream of Christianity has resisted the lure of the pure apocalyptist and insisted that the sure hope of the kingdom does not mean that the present can be written off. Along with the great vision of all things brought into a unity in Christ, has gone, even in the New Testament, those sober little lists of personal and social duties. The first fruits of the coming kingdom have here and now to be recognized amidst all the imperfections and loose ends of this world. The prophet continues to pursue his vocation for, as we attend to the everyday, we easily get stuck in the rut of the world and complacently settle down. The demands of the kingdom have to be held before us both by the words of the prophets and by holy lives, so that we recognize that our every effort and step forward is under the judgement and mercy of God. Because there is judgement, there can be no settling down in the illusion that we have arrived at the kingdom and, because there is mercy, we are kept hopeful, knowing that there is both the forgiveness of God for failure and that, even now, the forces of the age to come are at work making possible real, though imperfect, embodiments of that kingdom.

A free church could be a selfish church, using its freedom to escape from responsibility to society. Whether established or disestablished, the church has no immunity from sin. Yet if we serve the nation with the integrity of the gospel, we are less likely to find ourselves amongst the crowd of court prophets than with the prophet Amos. The state's response to such a church is likely to be that of Amaziah to Amos: 'O seer go away to the land of Judah and eat bread there and prophesy there; but never again prophesy at Bethel, for it is the king's sanctuary and it is the temple of the kingdom.' And then we shall have, with Amos, to learn to be without a privileged role in society, content simply to depend on the word which God has spoken. 'I am no prophet, nor a prophet's son; but I am a herdsman, and a dresser of sycamore trees, and the Lord took me from following the flock and the Lord said to me "Go, prophesy to my people Israel."' (Amos 7:14—15)

The Church of England has a distaste for conflict with the state and that is understandable, for who would have conflict where there is none? But so strong is this distaste that conflict will not be faced when it is there. Gallant though the Board for Social Responsibility's working party was, less edifying was the hustle of its parent body and of other leading churchmen to disown its report. Honest disagreement was legitimate and indeed healthy, but the anxiety to smooth things over and show there was no conflict between church and state less so. There are particular reasons why churchmen should be jumpy about any further withering of the church—state links. The state is taking notice of the Church of England in a way which it never did twenty years ago. Indeed it may be that Parliament has no interest in possible rupture for, in the divided state of the country, a national church could prove more useful than nationalized railways. It would not be a matter of swinging the Church of England back to being 'the Tory Party at prayer', just that it should behave itself, concentrate on personal morality and provide the bromide of a soothing liturgy. The bonds of establishment could come alive again and the national church be given a useful and honourable place in society. It is a possibility not without allure for churchmen because, as we shall see, it offers the Church of England a purpose and identity at a time when it desperately needs both.

4 Establishment or Church Unity?

'The tide of history is running in the direction of disestablishment . . . but, of course, tides can be reversed.' It may be that we are seeing that reversal of the tide for which the late Bishop Ronald Williams hoped. The changing mood of the nation may now incline towards the establishment. The mood of the church has changed as well. After a period of theological questioning and uprooting, the Church of England takes more seriously its roots and worries about its identity. A mild liberal catholicism has given way to a reassertion of sharper party lines. Your typical young Anglican today is not likely to be a questing member of the Student Christian Movement but either an Evangelical with firm convictions and sure answers or, with far less show of theological seriousness, an Anglo-Catholic who turns from the perils of the mind to the comfort of the cult. In the middle, looking on in some bewilderment, is the now middle-aged angry young clergyman of the 1960s still feeding on the ever thinner liberalism of his youth, who sees with growing disillusionment his gentle dreams trampled by the rugged cohorts of the more doctrinaire. Division in the Church of England has been laid bare and deepened by debates over the ordination of women and plans for unity with the Free Churches. As we come to face the issues posed by the final report of the Anglican Roman Catholic International Commission (ARCIC), it looks as if there will be a similar polarization, with a new alliance between strict Evangelicals and liberals standing together in opposition to unity in this direction. If the unity of the nation is strained so too is that of the church, and might it not be that establishment will prove as necessary to the latter as it seems helpful to the former? It has been argued that establishment alone can hold together the bewildering variety of the Church of England. Thus the religious correspondent of *The Times*, Clifford Longley, exploring the question of the identity of the Church of England, claims that although both Evangelicals and Anglo-Catholics have clear ways of affirming this identity, neither can be described as providing 'home-grown Anglican confessionalism'. So he argues:

> Some structure must hold middle, high and low Anglicans together . . . and it is in fact the establishment of the church, its legal status in the nation and the constitution, that serves as the underlying principle of unity. It is just about the only thing all Anglicans have in common and the only thing that prevents them from fragmenting into a handful of small denominations. The unity of the Church of England is not, therefore, a product of religious faith, but of law, history and politics; and it is undoubtedly a great asset that its unity is thus protected from internal religious tension. It means however that the Church of England has to observe the terms and obey the limits of the unwritten social contract between itself and the state. . . If it derives its unity from its establishment, hence from the state, there is a sense in which its authority too is dependent on the state.[79]

That puts, with characteristic frankness, a belief which many would share but be too delicate to express, that establishment alone holds the Church of England together. Behind the synodical wicket-keeper stands the parliamentary long-stop which, in the providence of God, checks our divisiveness. Whatever this party or that may say, there remains laid up the Book of Common Prayer enshrining the standard of faith and far out of reach of the itching hands of reforming zealots. We recall Mr Enoch Powell's words in 1974: 'The church owes this, its comprehensive character, to the very fact that its formulae and its liturgy, being established by the law of Parliament are peculiarly rigid and difficult of change.'[80] Thus there are those who, with Mr Powell, would argue that establishment is part of the very identity of the Church of England. Without paying overmuch attention to those churches of the Anglican Communion which exist without such ties with the state, they believe that through disestablishment we would lose things essential to the English Reformation, something of that refusal to allow clerics to rule the roost, something of the rugged independence of a national church. The Church of England disestablished would be a different creature, a mere denomination, less congenial to the theologically lively, altogether less varied and interesting.

It is argued that establishment both shields us from a self-destructive search for identity and itself remains part of that identity. Peel away this skin and, as with the onion, you might find it hard to stop. It would be possible thus to ward off disturbing questions about the identity of the Church of England were we able to pursue our vocation as the national church in isolation from other churches. But we are not. Our recognition of these churches and our search for unity with them makes such evasive inaction impossible. In any serious search for unity these other churches need to know where the Church of England stands. Ecumenism is not a game to be played with masks on but a dialogue in which we need to see one another as we really are. Two schemes for unity, one for organic unity with the Methodist church, the other for covenanting with the Methodist, Moravian and United Reformed churches, have now foundered on the Church of England's inability to state, on a number of crucial issues, where it, rather than the parties within it, stands.

Whatever one may think about these schemes, and for the author the first seemed good because, after careful search for common faith, it aimed clearly at the goal of organic unity while the second seemed not so good because it did not do these two things, yet failure in both cases was caused by our church's inability to come to a common mind. The Church of England with its comprehensiveness has looked on the surface a promising model for ecumenism, but in practice it has turned out to be something of a time-bomb, liable to blow up in the face of any concrete proposals for union. Why is it that we have become an ecumenical liability? Because, although we have managed to comprehend much variety, we have failed to unite it. In a spirit of 'live and let live' we have existed in a state of practical congregationalism, with various party-labelled churches each claiming to be 'the real Church of England'. Father Biretta has persuaded his congregation that 'real' Anglicanism is Anglo-Catholic, Canon Northend has claimed the same for his Evangelical party, while the Very Reverend Pig-in-the-Middle has, with even greater plausibility, persuaded the faithful that 'no extremes and decent moderation' is the genuine article. We have mistaken this lazy comprehensiveness for unity, and in doing so have caused much hurt to our ecumenical partners. If we are to build up rather than break down, we shall have to end the game of clapping the telescope to the blind eye when we look at other members of the Church of England. All this variety is in fact what the Church of England is, and our task is, not to pick from the menu what takes our fancy, but to allow ourselves to be confronted by and learn from it all. The Reformation in England placed on our agenda the task of showing that catholicism and evangelicalism belong together, that the critical use of the mind and the warm devotion of the heart need one another. If we cannot take up this task then Anglicanism has no reason to exist and not even the fig-leaf of establishment will hide our nakedness. The mysterious thing is that through ecumenism, the very call to die to separate Anglican existence, we are being pressed into fulfilling our Anglican vocation. It is by engaging whole-heartedly in the search for unity whose aim is the loss of separate identity, that we shall find ourselves.

It sounds paradoxical and unnerving but it has the mark of him who calls us to die in order that we may live. Full-blooded ecumenism, what we used to call the search for 'organic unity', requires institutional death. It was the absence of any smell of death in the covenanting scheme, the clinging on to the last vestiges of our peculiar institutional lives, which made some of us see that it was inadequate. Unity by stages, as in the old Anglican-Methodist scheme, was realistic and acceptable but only in the context of a clear commitment to the goal of organic unity. Slipping into a less demanding federalism or being content to become better neighbours on 'dropping in' terms, was not enough. There had to be expressed the straightforward desire no longer to be Anglicans, Methodists or members of the United Reformed Church, but simply to be Christians in a deeper, richer and more balanced way. For the Church of England the question of identity will be answered neither by a return to party ghettoes nor by leaning on the broken reed of establishment, but in advancing resolutely along the path to unity, sitting with our fellow Christians to attend to the Word of God and allowing our corporate life to be shaped by that Word.

At great moments in the past the church has rediscovered its identity by being rediscovered by the gospel. Two Church of England doctrine commissions have reported on Christian belief: one, *Christian Believing* (1976), moved quickly from an attempted agreed statement of faith to a number of individual credos; the other, *Believing in the Church* (1981), corrected this appearance of individualism and studied the corporate nature of faith. At some length it was shown that belief cannot be a private matter 'between myself and God', and that here too 'no man is an island.' Yet this cautious attempt to discover the common faith of the Church of England was combined with a marked reluctance to say what it is. Questions about 'how' we believe and 'where' we believe were answered, but hardly 'what' we believe. The task is by no means easy and we are tempted to make a virtue out of necessity by erecting the Anglican reluctance to define into the one essential dogma. Although 'proclaiming the truth' is seen as a Christian obligation, it is asserted that:

the definition of doctrine by an act of authority for the

whole of the church concerned should be an event so rare as to be almost unthinkable. . . To define draws a line around part of the Christian community, giving confidence, maybe, to those inside the newly drawn circle, releasing them from their doubts and perplexities. But however much this sort of mental consolation, sometimes called certainty, is yearned for, is it really calculated to help us to progress in our Christian living and thinking?[81]

Professor Jack McManners writes: 'The Church of England does not indulge in ringing, authoritarian, doctrinal formulations.'[82] The commission agrees: 'doctrine should be authoritatively defined as little and seldom as possible.' Implicit doctrine is thought to be better than explicit doctrine, for 'beliefs that are expressed only by implication are less exposed to incredulity and correction and, on the contrary, are invested with the mystique of custom and ceremony, and so outlast the changes that take place at the level of argument and knowledge.'[83] Indeed 'a church which still values establishment, in the sense of a conscious responsibility for the nation, must inevitably express its beliefs more by implication than by explicit confessional formularies and be singularly disinclined to excommunicate or deprive for heresy.'[84]

Now 'definition' of doctrine is a very ugly notion if it implies that we can adequately grasp the Word of God and hold it, as it were, in a container. God is reduced to a mere notion and we are tempted to imagine that he is caught in the net of our propositions, and so under our control. The doctrine commission is right to be sensitive to the harm which such pocketing and manipulation of God has done. It is the source of arrogance, the breeding ground of a persecuting spirit. There is thus a right reaction against 'poor talkative little Christianity', a godly desire to get away from a strident, over-confident dogmatism which would pound its victims as with a sledge-hammer, a shrewd scepticism about the activities of word-spinning theologians. Who has not stood in a theological library and felt the gulf which yawns between this mountain of words and the voice of the Man of Nazareth? If we dare to speak, it is from silence that we must do so and to silence swiftly return.

Yet, if the word 'definition' is loaded with such objectionable overtones, the word 'articulation' may prove both less emotive and quite essential to the nature of our faith. Christianity is a religion of articulation. 'How are men to call upon him in whom they have not believed? And how are they to believe in whom they have never heard? And how are they to hear without a preacher? . . . Faith comes from what is heard and what is heard comes by the preaching of Christ.' (Romans 10:14,17) Christianity is about 'the mystery hidden for ages and generations but now made manifest' and this carries the obligation to make the Word of God fully known, 'to make known how great are the riches of the glory of this mystery, which is Christ in you, the hope of glory.' (Colossians 1:26,27) It is necessary to be quite clear about this. Christians are not in business to air their religious speculations drawn from the slender resources of spiritual insight and intellectual ability, but to articulate the gospel because God has articulated himself in Jesus. We are driven into the difficult and dangerous task of hammering out words by the Word of God. 'The lion has roared; who will not fear? The Lord God has spoken; who can but prophesy?' (Amos 3:8) Although the word we speak remains a human and therefore inadequate word, others are able to receive it 'not as the word of man but as what it really is, the Word of God' (1 Thessalonians 2:13). Because of the Lord, the Holy Spirit, the church as 'pillar and bulwark of the truth' (1 Timothy 3:15) can be trusted to go on confronting men and women with living and saving Word. This does not mean that God is enclosed in the box of our words or that we have reduced his mystery to a slogan. We have not grasped God, we do not yet see face to face, but only puzzling reflections as in a mirror. Christian articulation and communication depends on God's grasping our words and making them the servants and instruments of his Word.

When therefore the pressures of the ecumenical movement make it necessary to state where we stand, we are not fearfully to draw back from expressing the faith that is in us. Of course ecumenism involves the institutions and structures of the church, not only because we live in this world and not in the heavenly Jerusalem, but because the Word, being made flesh, comes to dwell amidst such social realities. The whole movement of the Incarnation is from the invisibility of God to his manifestation in the flesh, and in that movement we are caught up. The church has to be bodied forth as one thing, the sacrament of Christ, which is why its divided denominational state is a standing denial of the gospel and why we are to stay on course in our commitment to organic unity. But the starting point is not with institutions, shared church buildings, common organs of consultation or even bishops as the bond of unity. To start at this end is to lay ourselves open to the accusation that ecumenism is nothing more than the merger of institutions for the sake of self-preservation in a hostile world. The institutional exists for the sake of the common faith which is to inhabit and animate it. Our commitment to organic unity is not for the sake of administrative convenience or good fellowship but for the sake of the gospel. The question of common faith cannot thus be dodged in the way the report on the proposals for covenanting made it appear to be dodged. This is assuredly not a matter of setting one another examination questions in the spirit of the hostile examiner eager to catch the candidate out, and that in a very narrow range of contentious subjects. There should be joy in confessing the faith which we already share, joy in digging beneath the polemical language of the past and discovering the solid ground of common faith. It is an arduous and costly task in which the participants, because they seek beyond the old slogans a new way of speaking, will be accused of betraying the past and fudging the issues, and yet, as the old Anglican-Methodist Commission and ARCIC have shown, it is possible to lay foundations upon which we may securely build. A fastidiousness about 'definition' must not be allowed to inhibit us from continuing along this path. When ecumenical partners labour to answer each other's question 'where do you stand?' progress is made.

For Anglicans to answer this question faithfully means doing justice to both the roots and the developments of the Church of England. We cannot cut ourselves off from our roots or deny that this past is still part of us. Every tradition has its 'monuments', those decisive articulations of the past to which the adherent has to remain faithful to be part of that tradition. Such 'monuments' are more than ancient relics; they continue to exercise an influence on the present. For the Church of England the Book of Common Prayer and the Thirty-Nine Articles are such monuments, so that, to be a member of it, is to be part of a community which once articulated where it stood in this particular way. Of course we share in a stream of life which did not stop in the sixteenth century, so that to be faithful to the past as an Anglican is also to accept it in all its variety and seeming contradiction, to learn to live with the faith of the Reformers as much as with that of the Caroline divines, to take Latitudinarians along with Evangelicals and the fathers of the Oxford Movement.

But if roots are important, so too is development, the continuing life of the Church of England. It is easy to fall over into an idolatry of the past, or at least one segment of it, and thereby to dodge the task of attending to the Word of God in our own situation. In the end we must ask not 'what does the Book of Common Prayer teach?' but 'what do we, living in the tradition of which the Book of Common Prayer was a decisive articulation, but here and now ourselves confronted by the living Word of God, Jesus Christ, see as the truth of the matter?' Because our loyalty to this tradition is not that of sticking in a stagnant pool but moving with the flowing stream, it is a critical loyalty. Led by the Holy Spirit who guides into all truth, we have as much freedom and duty as our forefathers to articulate the faith that is in us. Without going back on the past we can recognize that its articulations of the faith have often been lopsided and inadequate. A fundamentalist approach to our 'monuments' of faith is neither faithful nor satisfying to those who ask, not where Anglicans stood in the sixteenth century, but where they stand now.

In fact of course the doctrine of the Church of England has developed. Certain liturgical practices, like the Commination Service, have, for instinctive doctrinal reasons, been quietly dropped, the Alternative Service Book Baptism expresses an understanding of original sin which is different from that in the 1662 book, and the new eucharistic prayers are open to a richer and less negative understanding of the relationship between the Cross and the sacrament. Indeed the whole case for the ASB rests upon a conviction that such development represents a truer understanding of the revelation of God in Christ and its implications than that of the 1662 book. Judge the new services in terms of the updating of language in order to entice the man on the Clapham omnibus into church, and you will be hard put to mount a convincing case. The language is often banal and pitiful, and there is as little evidence that it attracts the crowds as there is that the language of the Prayer Book attracts them. The case to be made out is that the new services express better theology. Much as I love the language of Cranmer and find that, as Sunday by Sunday I celebrate his liturgy, my Anglican roots are kept alive, yet I am bound to confess that I am irritated by its man-centredness, its ommission of central features of the saving action of God in Christ and its indulgence in anti-Catholic polemics in the prayer of consecration. Is it not to be deplored that whenever our eyes are directed Godwards we have to keep interrupting this outward movement of worship with an ever-renewed return to our human unworthiness? Having confessed our sins, been absolved and reassured with comfortable words, we ascend to cry 'Holy, holy, holy', only to be bumped back again to contemplate our unworthiness to so much 'as to gather up the crumbs under thy table'. Is it not puzzling that in the eucharistic prayer there is mention neither of the Incarnation of our Lord nor of his Resurrection, whereby alone he is able to make himself known to us in the breaking of the bread? And is it not regrettable that much of the prayer of consecration is taken up with the negative insistence that the sacrament we celebrate is no repetition of Calvary? Despite its linguistic barbarism, it is to Rite A of the ASB that I turn for a sounder and richer theology. These reflections of one who celebrates Cranmer's liturgy every Sunday and who appreciates this experience, are given only to show that, although we may argue that the theology of ASB has its roots in the book of 1662, it undoubtedly registers a development.

Now the trouble is that this frank recognition of development is inhibited by the Worship and Doctrine Measure's laying up of the Book of Common Prayer in the hands of Parliament. Archbishop Michael Ramsey believes that this

is a necessary condition for the privileged position of the church in relation to the state. If the state gives privilege to one particular church, it must know the identity of that church — in this case a church that is definable Anglican and not one which might decide at will to be Calvinist or Roman Catholic. The place of the Prayer Book as a visible standard, which may be used when it is asked for, is a mark of the church's identity.[85]

Now, of course, the Church of England must always treat the Prayer Book as a classical and normative document but any suggestion that this is dependent on parliamentary custodianship is shown to be false by the fact that other Anglican provinces have registered doctrinal development in revised prayer books and yet retained the 1662 book as a doctrinal guide. Indeed the Worship and Doctrine Measure seems to have elevated the 1662 book to a quasi-canonical status along with the Bible. As Mr Powell said, with approval, this gives to the Church of England a framework of peculiar rigidity. In the context of ecumenism it could be the rigidity of rigor mortis. If it appeared to the state that the Church of England by entering into communion with the Church of Scotland was 'going Calvinist', or by entering into communion with the Roman Catholic church was 'going Roman Catholic', would not this form of defining the Church of England's identity be a hindrance to union? Ecumenism demands that we advance beyond being 'definable' Anglicans and become Calvinist, Lutheran and Roman Catholic as well. Be that as it may, ecumenical dialogue requires churches which have voices able to express with authority how they now understand their traditions. As we have seen in the debate on the Prayer Book Protection Bill, some parliamentarians are not willing to grant that the General Synod can be the official spokesman of the Church of England. Time and again peers denied that it could speak for the 'real' national church.

The Church of England thus appears to be without a clear authoritative voice at precisely the moment it most needs one. Its 'word' is officially enshrined in a carefully guarded book whose parliamentary custodians, although capable of being stirred to defend the rights of the nation to have that book used in divine worship, show no inclination or ability to declare what it might stand for. This matters because it is in churches putting questions and answering questions that we make ecumenical progress. Thus Anglicans have wished to question Roman Catholics about the papacy and we have received answers which are helpful and, on the whole, reassuring. These answers register a development in the thinking of the Roman Catholic church. The affirmations of Vatican 1 have not been rejected but some of the unfinished work of that council has been taken up by Vatican 2, so that the official mind of the Roman Church now speaks of the papacy in the context of collegiality with other bishops. The ability to articulate development and to achieve clearer definition, far from being the restrictive drawing of lines which some Anglicans fear, has proved liberating and creative. We are now moving into a position where we want to respond to this. If we are simply locked up in the definitions of our past, tied to the unalterable doctrine of the Book of Common Prayer and the Thirty-Nine Articles, there would be little prospect of a positive response. 'The Bishop of Rome hath no jurisdiction in this realm of

England' (Article 37) — the Church of England is by nature an independent national church which rejects the papacy. Any hope of unity with Rome depends on our ability to modify authoritatively this position. Indeed the *sensus fidelium* seems to be moving away from such nationalistic anti-papalism. The positive statements of the ARCIC documents have been backed by the warm welcome given by all, save a soured minority, to Pope John Paul II on his visit to this country. Moreover, it is now becoming apparent that the muddle into which the Anglican Communion has sunk over the ordination of women, with some provinces ordaining them and some not, was the result of unbridled local autonomy. The issue which confronted the 1978 Lambeth Conference was that of the extent and limitations of provincial autonomy. Although the bishops poured liberal doses of fudge on these troubled waters, their recognition of 'the autonomy of each of its member churches . . . to make its own decision about the appropriateness of admitting women to Holy Orders' was somewhat modified by the admission that followed 'that such provincial action in this matter has consequences for the Anglican Communion as a whole' and by its recommendation that no decision to consecrate women as bishops 'be taken without consultation with the episcopate through the primates'.[86] Although the door was being bolted after the horse had left the stable, it looks as if an important lesson was being learned. At the same time that the Anglican mind is opening to some form of papacy, it seems to be considering a modification of the autonomy of national churches.

There is still a long way to go if we are to achieve unity with Rome. Within the synods of the Church of England alone there are rough waters to be negotiated on the issue of authority, but surely a considerable part of the journey now lies behind us. It is possible to be a realist and still believe that the General Synod will finally accept the ARCIC documents. But this, quite apart from the attitude of Rome to the enterprise, would not be the end of the road for us in England. There is Parliament to be encountered and

93

formidable laws to be repealed and it is by no means clear that a Parliament into which spill the troubled waters of Ulster, would go along with the Synod's wishes. Members of Parliament will be in receipt of passionate letters from constituents and will finally have to decide whether this union be a development or deviation in the life of the national church. There is a constitutional minefield to be crossed. How could the Church of England enter into communion with a church when statute forbids its Supreme Governor to be reconciled or hold communion with that church? It is worth recalling that when some members argued that the passage of Worship and Doctrine Measure would ease the way to church reunion, Mr Enoch Powell replied in words sombre indeed to the ears of all ecumenists:

> More than the obstacle of the 1662 Prayer Book stands for the Anglican church, in the way of complete union either with the Free Churches or with Rome. It must cease to be an established church altogether, and the Queen must cease to be the Supreme Governor on earth of the Church of England, if the Church of England and the Church of Rome are to be one.[87]

In a recent essay Gordon Dunstan seems to agree with this view and, holding establishment to be of the *esse* of the Church of England, sees only the possibility of a union which falls short of being organic.[88] It will be clear that I too find Mr Powell's judgement realistic but, believing the priority to be obedience to the Lord who calls us to organic unity, can see no way to such unity save through disestablishment.

'Let us not cross bridges until we get to them.' There is a very understandable reluctance to face such problems which may be a long way off. The task to hand is to convince not only the synods of the Church of England but those of the other provinces of the Anglican Communion that this is an honest way forward. There will be time enough after that to bother our heads about Parliament. It is a counsel to which the author, ever willing to put off today what might never have to be done tomorrow, responds with every fibre of his being, and yet it will not do. The failure of two unity schemes shows that such easy-going pragmatism is not enough. Cheerful plodding on without looking round the next corner lulled both ourselves and our ecumenical partners into a false sense of security. The Church of England's shaming failure to come to a common mind owes something to the continuing presence of the Parliamentary long-stop. The synodical wicket-keeper becomes irresponsible and theologically lazy. If, at the end of the day, Mother Parliament will make our decisions for us, why summon the determination and patience to dig beneath our internal differences and come to a common mind? By continuing to live under the shadow of the Palace of Westminster, the Church of England retains an adolescent air, one minute stridently affirming its independence, the next scuttling back to nestle under the warmth of the establishment. Ecumenism requires maturity, churches that can stand on their own feet, sort out their own problems and make their own decisions about the future. Although in recent years the Church of England has gained greater freedom, it is on a lead which, as the debate on the Prayer Book Protection Measure showed, has a master at the end who is not wholly asleep. It is not an arrangement which encourages responsibility.

We need to be clear with ourselves and with our ecumenical partners what sort of unity we are really after. If it is of a federalist type as suggested by the covenanting scheme, then establishment could be encompassed, but if it is organic unity, the marriage of churches, then the church-state ties will have to be broken. Nobody can imagine that Roman Catholics will accept the sovereign as Supreme Governor of the Church or that Free Churchmen will acquiesce in even the lingering remnants of parliamentary control of worship and doctrine, let alone the Crown appointment of chief pastors. Which path we choose will be decisive for establishment, but choose we must.

There are subtler ways in which our ties with the state inhibit the move to unity. It is perilous to neglect the wounds which divided Christians have inflicted upon one another in the past.[89] Of course there is a destructive way of brooding on the past, an ungodly grief which we know feeds the violence of Ulster and which Englishmen tasted with shocked surprise when it overflowed in this land before the papal visit. But the answer to the past brooded upon is not the past ignored. The wounds we thrust away and will not face are those which most deeply infect the roots of our relationships. There is a remembrance which is necessary to repentance and new life. Anglicans find it hard to believe that their church, which holds them in such a kindly and tolerant embrace, could ever have been a persecuting church, excluding nonconformists and recusants from the life of the nation. Yet to our fellow-Christians establishment has meant civil disability, imprisonment and even death. Such bland blindness is shown when Anglicans fail to perceive how offensive it is to Roman Catholics that, although the heir to the throne is free to marry a Lutheran, Methodist, Muslim or Hindu, he is not free to marry a Roman Catholic. It seems such a minor point, only becoming a live issue when newspapers are agog with rumours of foreign princesses who are rarely Anglican, but laid to rest when the heir to the throne becomes safely married to a good and delightful Anglican. We are off the hook again. But precisely because the issue is no longer one which derives life from gossip over particular individuals, we should feel free to treat the matter on its merits and rid ourselves of a remaining link with an oppressive past. If we cannot repent of the sins of our forefathers, we can and should repent of our continued acquiescence in such sin.

There is a similar lack of historical sensitivity in our failure to understand the sharper criticisms of episcopacy made by some Free Churchmen. Kindly bishops, who often feel the imprisoned victims of committees and synods, find it incredible that fiercer members of the United Reformed Church can continue to treat them as eighteenth-century prelates. But this is to ignore the way the past is kept alive through the pressures of establishment. Anglicans are accustomed to say that the Church of England contents

96

itself with the fact of the historic episcopate while committing itself to no one theory. The absence of 'definition' is thought once more to be liberating. The stumbling block is imagined to be a 'pipe-line' theory of succession, which almost no one holds, while the asset is episcopacy as it is practised. Yet is this really so? Is not a theory which sees the bishop as the pastor of the pastors, the leader of a team of ministers, or as the teacher, the minister of the word, whose succession in the episcopate is a sign of the church's apostolic succession in faith, precisely that to which an evangelical tradition can respond? Is it not the practice which is so often the stumbling block? This is not to suggest that there are many prelatical tyrants around but a lot of tired, overworked men who find it hard to give top priority to that for which they were consecrated. Although some things laid on the backs of bishops stem from that lamentable burgeoning of ecclesiastical machinery which followed in the wake of synodical government and others from their own inability or unwillingness to delegate responsibility, the main burden is simply the absurd size of most dioceses. That the theory has not been embodied is shown by the fact that suffragan and assistant bishops are needed thus making a nonsense of the bishop as the 'focus of unity'. It is not really amazing that some Free Churchmen are unenthusiastic about taking such a manifestly distorted ministry into their systems.

Although the obvious is repeated time and again that there should be smaller dioceses, the obvious is consistently ignored. We are headed off by the feeblest of arguments. How could small dioceses afford to staff a central office? How could they afford a cathedral complete with dean and chapter? Yet if we are serious in wanting bishops, that is pastors of the pastors and teachers of the faith, the case for the small diocese defined by the number of priests a bishop can really know and effectively lead, and the number of parishes to which he can genuinely be a teacher, is unanswerable. At least if we cannot have episcopacy like that, one is inclined to agree with Free Churchmen that there is not much point in having it. Yet the unanswerable is

97

met by the dead bat of establishmentarianism which, despite the clear gospel injunction to avoid the world's model of leadership, has its own picture of bishop as 'top man' or 'national figure'. Indeed it is on such an understanding of the status of a bishop that Gordon Dunstan justifies the continued involvement of the Crown in their appointment: 'Are bishops and deans still to be men of such stature, and their offices still of such significance, that they count for something in the national life? that it matters who shall occupy these positions? If so the crown is the apt embodiment of that national interest.'[90]

Indeed it is often said that we could not expect the Crown to interest itself in the jumped-up rural deans which the multiplication of dioceses would require. The bishop, we are told, is not only a bishop in the church but potentially one who will take his seat in the House of Lords. Such remarkable arguments, paraded with an ungodly deference for 'highflyers', are thought sufficient to sink those wild evangelical dreams of a teaching and pastoral episcopate. It is little wonder that Free Churchmen continue to sniff with suspicion at the historic episcopate and fail to see it as the gift of Christ we claim it to be. No wonder, in the debates on the covenanting proposals, that some Free Churchmen gave the impression of a grudging willingness to accept episcopacy, not because they were convinced that this was a gift of Christ to be shared, but because Anglicans were hooked on this eccentricity and, for the sake of unity, here was a bitter pill to be swallowed.

When we are reduced to such joyless bargaining — 'we will take your bishops if you will admit that our non-episcopally ordained ministers are true ministers of the gospel' — we can be sure that the search for Christian unity has taken a wrong turn. The sure mark of true ecumenism is the conviction that we are turning with joy to Christ to receive from his hands even more than he has, in his mercy, given us in our separation. There has to be a readiness to share all that we are convinced Christ has given to us and a willingness to receive all that he has given in the lives of our fellow-Christians. The search for unity is for a richer

Christian life and in it we jettison only our negations. Of course what each church has to offer does not always look like a divine gift for, in our hands, it has become encrusted with sinful distortion. Reformation of our separate traditions thus becomes a necessary part of ecumenism. Renewal by the Word of God has been the cry of the Reformation churches yet it is sobering to face the fact that the most far-reaching example of this in practice has been the Second Vatican Council of the Roman Catholic Church. Here was a deliberate placing of the church under the judgement of God's self-disclosure in Christ. The consequences of such reformation for ecumenism have been enormous. Beliefs and practices of the Roman Communion which had once appeared only as barriers to unity are now seen by the churches of the Reformation in a new light. We have been able to glimpse the gifts of Christ which before had been hidden by the distortions of sin. All churches need the same reformation so that the variety and richness of Christian life, instead of being lost in a grey uniformity, can be seen and accepted as part of the fuller and more balanced faith which our Lord is offering to all members of his body.

If the Church of England has something of a crisis of identity on its hands, it needs to be remembered that, although such crises call for bold and resolute action, their effect is often the reverse, driving us back into some security of the past. Having failed twice in its search for unity, a weary church might think safety to be more precious than freedom. Let us be content with the privileges and disabilities of being the national church. Once snap the ties with the state and we could be catapulted into a dangerous unknown future; perhaps this diverse body would come to bits at its seams. Clifford Longley in his article 'Poles apart in the Church of England', admitted that there was an alternative to the church's deriving its unity from establishment and to depending for its ultimate authority on the state: 'The alternative, which may be the more honest course but which would be most unwelcome to Anglicans at large, is to sever the link and let the mould be broken, so letting the different components of the Anglican mixture seek their own confessionalism where they want to find it.' We have argued that just such a severing of the link and breaking of the mould is involved in serious ecumenism. However this does not envisage a scattering of the Anglican components but a moving together forward into a fuller unity. The bonds which bind Anglicans together are deeper and subtler than many Roman Catholics like Clifford Longley imagine. The existence of the Anglican Communion shows this. The alternative is not establishment or disintegration but, with a deep love and gratitude for our past, a dying to separate Anglicanism and a rising to life in that unity which is our Lord's will for us.

If we were to take the alternative route and bolt back into the safety of our establishment, the prospects for unity would be bleak. We would find ourselves, with the leader writers of the newspapers, applauding the growth of greater friendliness and toleration between the churches, but turning away from what we might come to call church 'mergers'. We could justify this by deploring any ironing out of the rich variety of Christian experience and by discovering a new value in denominationalism. 'Let these differences be preserved', we might argue, 'albeit in a liberal and kindly spirit. Let us be better friends, even tear down the fences between our houses so that we could become closer neighbours, but let us not venture to set up house together. If the lust for organic unity could be curbed, the churches would offer the nation an even wider range of religious goods from which the individual could pick according to taste.'

When one considers the uphill task of ecumenism and the demands it makes on the churches to reform their separate lives, such a modified goal is clearly attractive. We could live with differences of belief rather than labour to reconcile them. We could keep our establishment rather than face the upheaval of dispensing with it. It would be a possible and tempting option were we able to believe that the church is simply a club for god-seekers, a human association for the promotion of religion and morals, but if we cannot get away from the conviction that it is all this and more, if the church

100

be based, not on our views about God, but on his revelation of himself in Christ Jesus, then we cannot but be committed to the search for a common understanding of that revelation and its implications, for one church based on one Lord, one faith, one baptism. It is a harder path, because finding that new life in unity requires an institutional dying, but it is the only way to discover our true identity in Christ.

Conclusion: A Fuss about Nothing?

To have written on such an important topic as church and nation and then to have chosen to focus on the question of establishment will seem to many to be creating a fuss about nothing. Those who continue to value the establishment will not share this view, although they have sometimes given the impression that a damping down of discussion on this subject is the wisest form of defence. By and large the English are happy to accept what is there without too much questioning. Safety lies in discreet silence. Many others are more detached from what they consider to be a non-issue and deplore only time and energy consumed on it when there are other more important questions to be tackled. I have sympathy with this view. How a church, which is genuinely open to the world, can retain its Christian identity — how Christian witness in our society can be both sharp and effective — how the obstacles to Christian unity can be overcome: these I grant are the real questions and I grant furthermore that they will not be answered by the mere disengagement of the Church of England from its ties with the state. Disestablishment is, in truth, no cure for all ills. And yet I find that, as I explore these questions, I keep tripping over an obstacle in the way. That obstacle is the establishment, the particular laws which bind the Church of England to the state and the special status which these laws create.

In looking for an open church which has integrity, I find establishment tripping us into the pit of a phoney openness. In looking for prophetic simplicity and political involvement, I find establishment plunging us into a middle region

102

neither seriously prophetic nor political and imposing a model of Christian service which is inappropriate in a pluralist society. In looking for the union of our separate churches in one body, I find establishment checking our advance and tempting us to aim for a less ambitious goal. For the sake of the really important things for which we long, the obstacle must be removed.

'Disestablishment is itself a negative formula. It says what should be discarded. It would be better to ask *quo tendimus*? What is it the church should do and be different from what it does and is at the present? If the doing of it calls for the altering of parts, or the whole, of the state relationship, then we should be ready to pay the price.'[91] With these wise words of Archbishop Ramsey, I am in complete agreement. What should the church do? Prophesy and engage in the political task. What should the church be? An open church united in the affirmation of one faith. It is only for the sake of the renewal of the church in holy catholicity, in apostolic service and in unity, that disestablishment makes sense.

I have not dealt with the question of how these ties with the state can be broken. At this stage in the argument, the horrors of disendowment are normally paraded. Money speaks and can silence a good many arguments. I have little to say on this save to point out that in the cases of the Irish Church and the Church in Wales, the steam for disestablishment was generated by fairly hostile forces outside the churches in question. Disestablishment was thrust upon these churches. What I have sought is something different, a demand for disestablishment by the Church of England itself. I hazard the guess that this could make a lot of difference to the way in which disendowment was handled. It might be that, in the absence of bitterness and strife, a sensible bargain could be struck whereby the church's endowments were diverted from the payment of the clergy to the maintenance of its historic buildings which would remain both treasures and assets of the nation. Increasingly the living church is having to pay for the services of the living church and it would not be a vast step to take on the whole task if it were, at the same time, freed from the burden of caring for ancient buildings.

But all this requires, on the part of the church, a strong conviction that disestablishment is the right course. At the moment this conviction does not exist, indeed the tide seems to be turning both in church and nation in favour of establishment. Throughout the argument I have been painfully aware of choosing an inopportune moment to mount it. There is a lot to be said for sitting back, holding one's peace and awaiting the next turn of the tide. And yet when I consider what is at stake, what great movements the establishment hinders, I am encouraged to try to reopen the argument. The Church of England is not good at facing up to issues which stare it in the face. There was a moment, a few years ago, when the issue of establishment did just this. Those negotiating with the party political leaders for a new system of appointing bishops returned with the message that if establishment were retained the church could have no more than a greater say in these appointments; only if it were disestablished could it have what it had requested, the decisive voice. Then the issue to be or not to be, establishment or not, was there to be faced. It was not. The Synod was in a mood to prefer half the cake rather than the whole.

I have no further ambition for this little tract than that it might help to place the establishment of the Church of England back on the agenda. Indeed if it would but provoke those who believe in establishment to reach for their pens and show where I have been mistaken, I would be content. If the establishment be good for the church and for the nation, then show us how it is good and what are the firm links between the church-state relationship and the good alleged. For serious and lively debate to arise on this topic would be no bad way of celebrating the hundred-and-fiftieth anniversary of Keble's Assize Sermon.

Notes

1 Report of the Archbishops' Commission, *Church and State*,
   Church Information Office, 1970, p. 2.
2 Z.N. Brooke, *The English Church and the Papacy*,Cam-
   bridge, 1952, p. 21.
3 Article 37 of the Church of England, 'Of the Civil Magis-
   trates'.
4 Act of Supremacy 1559.
5 P.D.L. Avis, *The Church in the Theology of the Reformers*,
   Marshall Morgan and Scott, 1981, p. 132.
6 Richard Hooker, *Of the Laws of Ecclesiastical Polity*, Book 8,
   1648.
7 Ibid.
8 Ibid.
9 Ibid.
10 Ibid.
11 Ibid.
12 P. McGrath, *Papists and Puritans under Elizabeth I*, Bland-
   ford Press, 1967, p.1.
13 Ibid., p. 14.
14 Claire Cross, *The Royal Supremacy in the Elizabethan
   Church* , George Allen and Unwin, 1969, p. 114.
15 Thomas Arnold, *Principles of Church Reform*, ed. M.J.
   Jackson and J. Rogan, SPCK, 1962, p. 116
16 Ibid., p.113.
17 Ibid., pp. 114–15.
18 Ibid., p. 166.
19 Ibid., p. 167.
20 F.D. Maurice, *The Kingdom of Christ*, Macmillan, 1883, vol.
   2, p. 232.
21 Ibid., p. 301.
22 Ibid., p. 307.
23 Ibid., p. 320.
24 Ibid., p. 325.

25 Quoted in A.R. Vidler, *The Theology of F.D. Maurice*, SCM, 1948, p. 191.
26 F.D. Maurice, *The Kingdom of Christ*, vol. 2, p. 297.
27 Ibid., p. 344.
28 W.G. Ward, *The Ideal of a Christian Church*, James Tooney, 1844, p. 109.
29 Ibid., p. 40.
30 Quoted in Georgina Battiscombe, *John Keble*, Constable, 1963, p. 301.
31 J.H. Newman, *Certain Difficulties felt by Anglicans in Catholic Teaching*, Longmans Green, 1885, vol. 1, p. 101.
32 Ibid., p. 105.
33 J.N. Figgis, *Churches in the Modern State*, Longmans Green, 1913, pp. 39–40.
34 Quoted in D. Nicholls, *Church and State in Britain since 1820*, Routledge and Kegan Paul, 1967, p. 183. On Figgis see D. Nicholls, *The Pluralist State*, Macmillan, 1975.
35 C. Gore, *Reconstruction of Belief*, John Murray, 1926, p. 968.
36 C. Gore, *Church and Society*, George Allen and Unwin, 1928, p. 152.
37 Ibid., p. 162.
38 *Church and State*, p. 19.
39 Ibid., p. 2.
40 Ibid., p. 65.
41 Hansard, vol. 882, no. 31, pp. 1666–77.
42 Hansard, vol. 419, no. 67, p. 634.
43 Hansard, vol. 419, no. 67, p. 437.
44 Hansard, vol. 419, no. 66, pp. 624–5.
45 *Church and State*, p. 81.
46 K. Rahner, *Mission and Grace*, Sheed and Ward, 1963, vol. 1, p. 36.
47 Hansard, vol. 419, no. 67, p. 638.
48 Hansard, vol. 419, no. 67, p. 630.
49 W. Ward, *The Life of John Henry Cardinal Newman*, Longmans Green, 1912, vol. 2, p. 460.
50 J.H. Newman, *Discussions and Arguments on Various Subjects*, Longmans Green, 1885, p. 212.
51 *Vatican Council II*, ed. A. Flannery, Costello Publishing Co., 1975, p. 904.
52 K. Rahner, *Theological Investigations*, Darton Longman and Todd, vol. 14, 1976, p. 286.
53 F. Maurice (ed.), *Life of Frederick Denison Maurice*, Macmillan, 1884, p. 408.

54   C. Houselander, *The Young Man*, quoted in *Let there be God*, The Religious Education Press, 1968, p. 124.
55   Rahner, *Theological Investigations*, vol. 14, p. 283.
56   Ibid., p. 291.
57   Rahner, *Theological Investigations*, vol. 16, 1979, p. 219.
58   Rahner, *Theological Investigations*, vol. 6, 1969, p. 396.
59   Rahner, *Theological Investigations*, vol. 14, p. 291.
60   *Vatican Council II*, p. 984.
61   Ibid., p. 357.
62   Ibid., p. 367.
63   Ibid., p. 739.
64   Ibid., p. 821.
65   Ibid., p. 919.
66   Ibid., pp. 367–8.
67   A.M. Ramsey, *Canterbury Pilgrim*, SPCK, 1974, p. 181.
68   K. Rahner, *Mission and Grace*, vol. 1, p. 32.
69   Ibid., p. 24.
70   Jean Pierre de Caussade, *Self-Abandonment to Divine Providence*, Burns and Oates, 1959, section 10.
71   Quoted in D. Jenkins, *Beyond Religion*, SCM, 1962, p. 123.
72   *The Times*, 26 October 1982.
73   The report of a working party under the chairmanship of the Bishop of Salisbury, *The Church and the Bomb*, Hodder and Stoughton and Church Information Office, 1982.
74   J.A.T. Robinson, *On Being the Church in the World*, SCM, 1960, p. 56.
75   Quoted in D. Jenkins and D. Edwards, *Equality and Excellence*, SCM, 1961, p. 21.
76   R.H. Tawney, *The Acquisitive Society*,Collins Fontana, 1961, p. 9.
77   F. Maurice ed., *Life of F.D. Maurice*, vol. 2, p. 32.
78   Ibid., p. 137.
79   *The Times*, 1 November 1982.
80   Hansard, vol. 882, no. 31, p. 1674.
81   A report by the Doctrine Commission of the Church of England, *Believing in the Church, The Corporate Nature of Faith*, SPCK, 1981, p. 213.
82   Ibid., p. 231.
83   Ibid., p. 144.
84   Ibid., p. 148.
85   A.M. Ramsey, *Canterbury Pilgrim*, p. 180.
86   Lambeth 1978 Resolutions 21 and 22.
87   Hansard, vol. 882, no. 31, p. 1677.

88 G.R. Dunstan, 'Corporate Union and the Body Politic', *Their Lord and Ours*, ed. M. Santer, SPCK, 1982, p. 129ff.
89 Santer, 'The Reconciliation of Memories' in ibid.
90 Dunstan, 'Corporate Union', p. 144.
91 A.M. Ramsey, *Canterbury Pilgrim*, p. 176.

Index

111